THREE
COINS

THREE COINS

DONN BENNETT

The EC Publishing LLC books may be ordered through booksellers or by contacting:

EC Publishing LLC
116 South Magnolia Ave.
Suite 3, Unit F
Ocala, FL 34471, USA
Direct Line: +1 (352) 644-6538
Fax: +1 (800) 483-1813
http://www.ecpublishingllc.com/

Ordering Information:
Quantity sales. Special discounts are available on quantity purchases by corporations, associations, and others. For
details, contact the publisher at the address above.

Printed in the United States of America

TO THE HONOR AND GLORY
OF OUR LORD AND SAVIOR
JESUS CHRIST
THROUGH WHOSE LOVE
HAVE COME THREE
VERY PRECIOUS BLESSINGS:
SARAH PARKER, BENNETT and SMITH

ACKNOWLEDGEMENTS

Although, this is a rather modest literary work, considering my very limited talent, my first and most significant acknowledgement is that I could not have accomplished even this much without the wonderful help and encouragement from my family and friends. So, it is with my deepest gratitude and true humility that I thank those who devoted considerable time and effort to make *Three Coins* possible.

My dear friend and able critic, Carole Lee, was the first to suggest that I convert the rough draft of a short Christmas story into a book. She even suggested the title and with her usual sharp red penciling she contributed her own thoughts and comments. If not for her it most likely would not have been written. Thank you, Carole.

Other most helpful advice and superb proof reading came from, sadly, my late, very talented sister-in-law, Anne Bennett, and my lovely niece, Susan Bennett, both of whom are exceptionally skilled in English grammar and its proper use. To you I am also indebted and most grateful.

In producing such a work, it is essential that scriptural integrity be both contextually and theologically maintained. I was assured of meeting these requirements by Glen Arnett, one of the finest Biblical scholars and teachers I have known. Glen, your encouragement, help and friendship are deeply appreciated.

My utmost appreciation and gratitude to Katherine Cheshire for her splendid illustrations, and to John Hooks and Jennifer Joseph for their obvious computer and graphic skills in placing and arranging those illustrations. Most definitely, their contributions made the finished product.

Of course, there have been others who gave much encouragement and support. To mention a few, I express my special thanks to John Vaughan, Nick Shimoda, Rosie Oates and her fantastic daughter, Liz Anne, who gave it the young adult stamp of approval. To all of you my heartfelt thanks

I would certainly be remise if I did not express a great big THANK YOU to EC Publishing LLC and its staff for publishing *Three Coins*.

To God Be The Glory!
Donn Bennett

FOREWORD

I began this book several years ago with a short Christmas story I prepared for a Sunday school class I was teaching. Since I read it aloud and had no thought of publishing it I did not pay much attention to the grammar, spelling, etc. However, in sharing it with my dear friend, Carole Lee, she suggested that I dress it up and make it into a short book for young people. It did not even have a title and Carole suggested the one I have used. Unfortunately, after I proceeded to work on the book, lightning took out my computer, and I had foolishly not saved anything except the few pages of my original draft. Naturally this setback was discouraging, and I forgot about it for two or three years. One day I happened to run across what was left of the story and for some reason I resumed working on it. A new computer has allowed me to finish it.

I intended this primarily for our older youth, but I do sincerely hope adults will read it as well. As is my right as an author, I have taken certain literary license in some instances, but I have tried to be as consistent with the scriptures as possible, relying almost exclusively on the 1611 *King James Version*. It is my hope for all who read it that it will stimulate their interest and prompt them to read the scriptures to learn for themselves the truths they contain.

One apparent inaccuracy, but one I consider justified and important, is changing Jesus' words on the Cross from the question, "My God, My God, Why Hast Thou Forsaken Me?" to the statement, "My God, My God, Thou Hast Forsaken Me." I believe both versions have the same meaning. The question presupposes that God has forsaken Jesus, the essential fact. Bearing the sins of the world Jesus was the personification of man's sinful nature. It is this sinful nature that utters the first cry, and sin, which God abhors, is what causes God to separate from it. But the next outcry, "Father, Into Thy Hands I Commend My Spirit," comes from Jesus' spiritual nature, and Christ's pure and perfect spirit is most acceptable to His Father. In brief, these two different expressions clearly demonstrate that Jesus was both human and divine.

The name Ethan is a Hebrew Biblical name and befits the chief character portrayed in the book. Its meaning is "strong, optimistic, solid and persevering." It is also related to being wise. King Solomon in his wisdom was compared to Ethan the Ezrahite. ". . . For he [King Solomon] was wiser than all men; than Ethan the Ezrahite and Heman, and Chalcol, and Darda, the sons of Mahol; . . ." (1 Kings 4:29-31). Another Ethan was a musician and generally credited with writing the 89th Psalm. There are a total of eight Ethans mentioned in the Bible, and it is still a very popular name for male children in modern times, being in the top 13 in 2007.

If young people are my primary audience, you might question my judgment in being so graphic in my description of Jesus' torture and crucifixion. I can only apologize for the necessity of it. Mel Gibson in his memorable movie, *The Passion of Christ,* understood very well the significance of the extreme pain and torment suffered by Christ. In our legal system it is often said that the punishment must fit the crime. As the most sin laden person who ever lived, divine justice demanded that Jesus' punishment be as severe as humanly possible. I believe everyone, young and old alike, should understand this. When we refer to Jesus' blood being shed for us we normally think of the crucifixion. Yet, by the time Jesus was nailed to the cross he had very little blood left. To fully comprehend how much blood He actually shed is very difficult. We speak of His "suffering and dying for us," but I'm afraid we tend to minimize His suffering.

1

It was cold that night, perhaps colder than it had ever been. For certain, it was the coldest Ethan could remember. Of course, he could not remember that many, having lived through only twelve winters; thirteen if he lived through this one. But Jesse, who was much, much older, vowed it was also the coldest night he could remember. Ethan did not know just how old Jesse was, but he knew Jesse was very old, even older than his father, more than forty years at least.

Not only was the night especially cold, there was something else that made it unusual, even special--something about the stars. There was no moon. Though the stars on such nights were always bright and looked so near, tonight they shone brighter and seemed even closer. Ethan felt they would be near enough to touch if only his arms were a little longer. He knew it was a wild fantasy and foolish even to try. Besides, the very thought of extending his hand and arm into the frigid air outside the heavy covering of his cloak sent a shiver through his body.

As if the sudden chill were a signal for more pleasant thoughts, he thought of the end of his watch when he could return to where the other shepherds were camped. He looked at the distant hillside and the small hollow where they were gathered around a blazing fire. The hollow itself provided good shelter from the wind, which at night swept severely across the open, treeless land. Ethan knew that, with such protection and the fire, the others were quite comfortable. He felt a twinge of envy, but also thought he felt warmer.

The sheep grazed during the day as best they could upon the sparse dry remnants of grass in the shallow soil. At night they huddled on the same ground in a large mass of white, wooly bodies. Unlike goats, which Ethan had also tended, sheep needed no shelter other than their thick, curly coats of wool which provided them all the warmth and comfort they needed. This scene was so enticing, so alluring, that Ethan imagined he was immersed in the sheep's fleecy softness and drifting off to sleep. Even though the thought was only imagined, like that of the campfire and touching a star, it posed such a warm, cozy prospect, he nourished it and smiled, really believing he was warmer.

2

In spite of the cold, the night was incredibly beautiful, and just being there and doing what he was doing meant he was being treated like a man, doing a man's job. For that he felt immensely proud. Becoming thirteen years old, a *bar mitzvah,* a son of the commandments, was the greatest event in his life. On that special day he reached manhood. Without any real celebration it just happened. However, in keeping with custom, on the Sabbath following his birthday he *was* given special recognition; he was allowed to read from the Torah and recite a blessing over the reading. Nothing else, but the feeling it aroused was tremendous. Just a day earlier, he was only a child, not responsible or accountable for what he did or didn't do. Up until that time his father had been fully responsible for his conduct and behavior. If he did wrong, his father bore the blame. Because he loved and respected his father he had always tried to please him, never doing anything to bring shame or dishonor upon him or his mother. Then, just over night, he was suddenly grown up, an adult, and though he hadn't grown at all and looked just the same, he felt different. There was a definite change in both his feelings and attitude, a real transformation in his life. He believed this was just the way God planned it and intended it to be. He was like a bird that one moment is unable to fly and then suddenly can and does, leaving its fledgling days behind forever. That was the way his life would be, like that of his father, grandfathers and all of his people as far back as anyone could remember. And he knew it was the only life he wanted. Thinking such thoughts gave him a wonderful feeling, and on this night, cold as it was, he felt perfectly content, willing to accept the challenges and dangers that were ever present in the lives of shepherds.

3

Suddenly, without any warning or sign whatsoever, he was abruptly jarred from his reverie by the most awesome sight imaginable! The heavens literally erupted into a blazing radiance, brighter than daylight, as brilliant as a lightning flash that doesn't pass. The effect was almost blinding, but when he shielded his eyes, he could see that this great light came from what looked like a huge star, fixed in the sky, and sharply illuminating all the surrounding pastures and hills. The sheep below looked much whiter, like large puffs of snow, and across the way he could easily see the other shepherds, standing like statues around their fire which had dwindled to a mere spark in the overpowering brightness.

Ethan felt no danger, and somehow, he knew that this great display of power around him was good. Even the sheep were not alarmed. They had awakened, but without the baaing or milling about as there usually would have been when something as sudden and dramatic as this had disrupted their world.

As Ethan was beginning to adjust to this magnificent phenomenon, something even more startling occurred. Up above him, at a height higher than the hilltops, a man appeared, suspended in the air and dressed in a long flowing white robe. He was exceptionally handsome and although his countenance also shone brightly, Ethan was able to see his face quite distinctly, which, though absolutely serene was exultant in unmistakable joy. Instinctively, he fell to his knees and folded his hands in prayerful submission. The angel, for in fact it was an angel, began speaking. Ethan would have expected to hear something like the booming roll of thunder, but the voice was easy to hear, perfectly clear and melodious, rippling with excitement as he announced:

Fear not, for, behold I bring you good tidings of great
joy, which shall

Be to all people. For unto you is born this day in the
city of David a

Saviour, which is Christ the Lord. And this shall be
a sign unto you;

Ye shall find the babe wrapped in swaddling clothes,
lying in a manger.

There were other instructions, and when the angel had finished, he was
joined by many, many more angels, their radiant beauty adorning all the
hills and filling the entire countryside. In great choral splendor they sang.
Oh, how they sang! Their voices swelled through the valleys and around
and over the hills, praising God and this Christ, this Saviour that the first
angel had told about. Ethan was not sure what it all meant, but he well
remembered the words they sang:

Glory to God in the highest and on earth peace, good
will toward men.

As suddenly as the angels had come they went away. They simply
vanished, leaving everything as though nothing had happened, except
for the magnificent star that remained, motionless in the heavens with its
blinding, unwavering light.

4

Ethan remained kneeling for some time, his mind reeling, his heart pounding, his emotions in turmoil. When at last he stood up, he shook his head to clear it and knew he did not want to be alone. In the distance he could make out the faint glimmer of the campfire and ran toward it as fast as he could. In only minutes he was at the camp, panting and greatly relieved to be back with the others. The others, to his surprise, did not even notice him. They were too busy babbling, all at once, very loud and mostly unintelligible. What Ethan *was* able to understand were their vehement denials of being afraid. The denials were so emphatic Ethan suspected just the opposite was true.

His father, Abel, who was not talking, stood to one side, tall and erect. As Ethan drew closer he could see his face, and Abel, who usually appeared somewhat serious, now seemed even more so.

After several minutes, the voices of the others subsided to more moderate tones and Abel spoke. As the recognized leader of the group, his opinions were always respected and his instructions usually followed without question. Now his leadership was to be tested.

"My good friends," he said, "I do not fully understand what we have just witnessed, but I do know we have been given a message from God. Why this message was given to us is a question I can not answer. Nevertheless, it has been delivered to us and is not only a message of something that has happened, but there are instructions for us to do something. The angel told us that in the city of David, which we all know is Bethlehem, a child has been born, a very special child, who is the Christ, our Saviour. Such wonderful news, that had I not heard it from an angel of God, I would not believe it. But we all saw the angel and heard his words, so can there be any doubt that this great event has taken place? I think not. We will, I trust, all agree on that. The other part of the message is that we are to go to Bethlehem and see this child and afterwards we are to go throughout this entire area and make his birth known to others. Do any of you think we should not do this?" No one answered. For a minute or two there was only silence.

Finally, it was Protheus who responded, "Well, Abel, I don't know. I'll admit this was quite an experience, but leaving our flocks and going into town to see this baby, and then spending no telling how much time telling other people about it--well, really, that sounds kind of extreme. We have our families to think about. Just to go off and leave everything I don't think is a good idea. Perhaps, just one or two should go in and see if the baby is there and then come back and report on what they've seen. If they find the baby, then we could decide what we might do. But for all of us to up and leave in the middle of the night? Well, I just don't think it's a good idea." Two or three murmured some agreement to this.

Then Josiah spoke, "Protheus, don't you realize that this was not just some other man talking to us? This was an angel of God! This was God Himself who gave us that message. I personally don't want to second-guess God, and if we do what you suggest, that's exactly what we'd be doing. I'll admit I was really afraid, and truthfully still am, but now that I think about it, this is a wonderful opportunity to serve our God. We all know what happened to the Prophet Jonah, when he chose not to obey God, so I'm in favor of going right now to Bethlehem and doing what God has directed."

Other voices joined in general assent to what Josiah had said, even more than those who appeared to side with Protheus. Again, Abel spoke, "All right, it appears we are somewhat divided on this. Perhaps I should have said how I felt about it to begin with, so I will now. There is no doubt in my mind that Josiah is right. We should do exactly what we have been told and I am starting right now. Any of you who will join me will be welcome, with one exception. I do not think God expects us to leave the sheep unattended. That would be irresponsible. Ethan, I will ask you to stay and watch over the sheep until we return. I realize this is a great responsibility, but I believe you are capable, and you would be of more use here tending our flocks than going with us."

Without saying so, Abel knew that Ethan, as young as he was, would have little effect in spreading the news of a baby who was proclaimed to be the Christ, the Saviour of the Jews. Ethan, of course, was deeply disappointed to hear his father's request, but he would not oppose him. Even though he now had equal standing, Abel was still his father and he would obey him. In an effort to conceal his true feeling, he simply replied, "Certainly, Father."

Ethan thought Protheus and his supporters might remain with him, but truthfully, he was glad to see them all leave together. This not only showed their unity was restored, but more importantly, it showed their unanimous trust in him.

5

Now he had to decide how to manage his task of caring for the sheep. He knew they would be all right until morning and due to the interruption of their sleep they would not be stirring as early as usual. In any event he would be ready for them. First, he would bring hay down from where it was stored among the rocks behind him and have it on hand when they awoke. After the long night they would be very hungry, and at this time of year, the provender was essential to sustain them. For the next two or three hours, Ethan was busy moving the bulky racks of hay to a convenient place where it could be easily distributed. Normally, it would have taken him much longer, but with the great star and its abundance of light he was able to move with virtual ease over the rocks. For this he thanked God and continued to thank Him as he moved up and down the rocky slope.

He had estimated what would be needed and had just brought down the last of it, when, to his amazement, there suddenly appeared coming over the ridge a procession of people mounted on horses and camels. Following them were other animals, heavily burdened with great bundles, piled high upon their backs. His heart began to race and his mind tried desperately to think of what he should do. The long caravan came closer, and, to his dismay, he realized it was coming directly toward him. There was really nothing to do except wait.

In a few minutes the first of the riders was only a few feet away, and, at that point, the rider raised his hand and the entire procession halted. The rider then came forward alone, riding so high upon the huge camel that, when it stopped, he loomed ominously above Ethan. In spite of this frightening spectacle Ethan did not fail to notice the fine, noble features of the rider and the richness of his clothing. Beautiful heavy folds of purple velvet fell about the rider and a huge gem sparkled from the large turban covering his head. Then when he spoke, all of Ethan's fears disappeared. Never had he heard a human voice so refined and so soothing.

The rider said to him, "Good shepherd, we are strangers from faraway lands. My two companions and I are known as Magi. We have spent most of our lives studying, attempting to understand the meaning of life and the nature of both God and man. To help our understanding we have devoted much of our study to the heavens and the stars. So it is that we have followed this wonderful star that now bathes us in its light to the town of Bethlehem. Tonight, we found a child, newly born, lying in the manger of a stable. Because of this event and all else we have learned; we believe this child to be the Christ who will be a Saviour of all mankind. We do not know when His salvation will occur, but we are certain that it will. We now wish to return to our own countries and pursue further studies concerning this matter. There are, unfortunately, those who would prevent our return. We have been warned they lie in wait for us somewhere along the route we came, so we must find another way, even if it is longer and more difficult. We understand there is a passage through these hills which would place us beyond our enemies. Do you know of such a passage?"

Ethan was very familiar with several such passages. In recent years Abel had taught him the intricate network of many hidden paths and mountain passes, which had been developed by King Solomon centuries before and used in times of war to move his military forces quickly and secretly against Israel's enemies. Since Roman rule and its oppressive domination, this strategic system was used only by shepherds and the bandits who roamed about, preying upon unprotected and unwary travelers.

Knowing of these dangers, Ethan spoke with caution and somewhat evasively. "Noble Sir," he said, "just tonight we shepherds also received a message about this child. An angel appeared to us and told us that the child is the Christ and we were to go to Bethlehem and see him. His instructions were so urgent, so persuasive, that my father and the others were compelled to obey. They have now gone to Bethlehem and left me to tend the sheep."

"Oh, yes," said the Magus, "they were there when we arrived and left before we did. I would think they would have already returned."

"Your Excellency," said Ethan, "I am sure they would have, except they were told to tell others about what all they have seen, and I do not expect them until much later today."

"I see," replied the Magus, "but do you know of such a way as I mentioned?"

"Exalted One, I do, but such a way is fraught with danger," Ethan warned. "There are many who live only to steal from those who travel these parts, and often, after the travelers have been robbed, they are killed."

"Thank you for the warning, kind shepherd, but our party is strong. We are quite able to defend ourselves against the usual band of marauders and thieves that lurk about. Only an army could overcome us, and that is all we fear. So I beseech you, good shepherd, if it is possible, please guide us to safe passage through these hills."

Ethan wanted to help them. There was a suitable path not far away, and although it intersected with several other trails and was steep and rough, after a few hundred yards, it led to a narrow pass; then it descended sharply to a little traveled road that was reasonably level and serviceable. This road would take them a great distance from where the Magus indicated their enemies lay in ambush. Ethan did not believe it would take long to reach the pass and less time for his return. Also, with the enhanced brightness of the great star they could move much faster and shorten the time even more. Reasoning in this way, and confident the sheep would be safe while he was gone, Ethan agreed to serve as their guide. He was offered a camel or horse to ride, but never having ridden either, he declined the offer. Anyway, he could move fast enough on foot.

Taking his position at the very head of the column, Ethan looked back at the long line behind him. As he began walking, knowing that all those people and animals were following him and depending on him, he could not help but feel somewhat important. Yet, once they reached the obscure trail and began their strenuous climb the feeling left him.

Just as Ethan thought, due to the good light, their movement, though difficult, was relatively rapid. Soon he and the Magus reached the narrow opening of the pass which lay between two great rocks. Along the way the Magus told Ethan he was known as Malthus and Ethan said he was "Ethan." After they entered the pass, Ethan and Malthus halted, as did the procession behind them. Then Ethan led Malthus the short distance through the pass and pointed out to him the trail below.

When Ethan finished his instructions, Malthus dismounted from his camel and asked Ethan to kneel with him in prayer. As they knelt, Malthus prayed to Almighty God, praising Him for His greatness and thanking Him for his deliverance from their enemies. He also thanked God for sending the young man, Ethan, to guide them to the right path away from their enemies. He prayed for God to richly bless Ethan and all of his family. Ethan, at first, felt again a twinge of self-importance, but this feeling also passed as he realized that nothing that had happened had been done on his own. He was merely God's instrument. Such realization was humbling, but it brought with it an awareness that this was a better feeling. In fact, it was much better.

Malthus gave Ethan three large gold coins, one from each of the Magi. Then he asked Ethan to take an oath that he would not tell anyone about what he had done or what he had seen. Ethan readily swore that he would not disclose any of these events to anyone, not even to his father. The truth was he didn't know how he could tell his father since he had left the sheep unattended while he led the Magi's procession up the mountain. The secret also meant he could neither spend the money nor show it to anyone else. Doing either would require an explanation. Much as he would like to tell someone, he knew he could not. All he could actually do was keep the coins in a safe place and wait.

He did know the coins were very valuable, but it would be some years before he would learn just how valuable they really were. Not only were they much larger than the aureus, the standard Roman gold coin, they were also pure gold, each one worth many shekels. Although he tried, he never learned the meaning of any of the inscriptions on them or even where they were made. The Magi had indeed come from far away lands.

Before Malthus remounted his camel to begin the steep descent down the mountainside, he bowed solemnly to Ethan and spoke a few words in a language Ethan did not understand. Assuming this was no more than a friendly farewell, Ethan said something in return and even made a sort of half bow. Then Malthus was gone and Ethan was almost running down the mountain, swiftly passing the other members of the procession as they called to him, thanking him for what he had done.

6

Ethan arrived at the camp with a light and happy heart and just in time. Daylight was slowly spreading across the landscape, and he could hear the low mutterings and baaing of the sheep as they began to awaken and move about. He went immediately to the stacks of hay and laid them out within easy reach of the sheep. Soon they were all gathered around the several piles, pushing and nudging each other in greedy efforts to satisfy their hunger.

After the last of the hay had been devoured and he was satisfied all the sheep had been fed, he then had the difficult task of taking them to the nearby stream for water.

Actually, they would drink from a large, rock lined pool fed by the stream, built by shepherds many generations before. The pool had been necessary because sheep will not drink from a flowing stream. Ethan thought of this as he singled out the dominant ram and prodded him with his staff toward the water, knowing the others would instinctively follow. He remembered another shepherd, King David, who had written the beautiful psalm that began with the words, "The Lord is my shepherd. I shall not want. He maketh me to lie down in green pastures. He leadeth me beside the still waters. . . ."

"There," he thought, "Even King David knew that sheep would only drink from 'still waters'." At least this was something that was the same as it had been hundreds of years before. Until last night he had pretty much thought that nothing really changed. Now, after all that had happened during those few hours, he no longer believed nothing had changed. Instead, he was convinced that during his lifetime he would see many changes. The prospect was not alarming, but exciting and promising, and gave him a sense of hopefulness. He looked up at the star, which in the broad daylight was not so intense, but still quite visible. He reflected further, "This is a sign from God, a sign of hope. It must be. It has to be." At that moment he wanted so much for his father and the others to return and tell him about this Christ they had gone to see.

About then he also realized he had not eaten. From the height of the sun he could tell it was around the sixth hour, midday, and he had not eaten since the evening before. He built up the fire and took out some bread and cheese and a flask of water. He surveyed the sheep which had spread out and were grazing as best they could in a fairly regular formation. Only a few had wandered since the early morning and he had quickly steered them back into the general vicinity of the others. Being satisfied they were still in good order, he gave thanks over the food and began to eat.

At the first taste he felt suddenly ravenous and swallowed large mouthfuls without much chewing. When it was all gone, he drained the flask and leaned back against a rock. Not only had he not eaten for many hours, neither had he slept. With food in his stomach and feeling fairly comfortable, he nodded drowsily and went to sleep.

Unfortunately, his slumber was soon broken by the noisy return of the other shepherds. Yet, even in his sleepy condition, he could tell it was not noise like before, but happy, joyful songs and prayerful praises, glorifying God and thanking Him for His wonderful blessings.

As the others surrounded him, still singing and praying loudly, Ethan became fully awake. He begged them to tell him what they had seen and done. Finally, Abel quieted them enough for him to speak. Never had Ethan seen his father so blissful. His whole expression was transformed. The seriousness was gone, replaced by a look of peace and absolute contentment. He spoke softly, his lips curved slightly in a warm, caring smile. His voice pulsed with emotion. He told Ethan about the baby, who was named Jesus, sent by Jehovah to save His people. Abel told Ethan all about Mary, the mother, and Joseph, her husband. He talked in detail about the three wise men, as he called them, and the fine gifts they brought for Jesus. He then described how they all went as far as they could and told others about what they had seen. People, he said, were very receptive. They all saw the great star and knew that something wonderful was happening. Abel confessed that he was sorry Ethan could not have been with them. Ethan told him it was all right, that it was a good experience and he had really learned a lot. He was very glad Abel did not ask him to elaborate.

7

They had to reorganize, set new watches and assign individual duties and responsibilities. It was all done in a rather dazed, uninterested manner, but nevertheless, it was done.

Ethan was assigned the watch beginning at midnight, to a place out of sight of the camp and further away than where he'd been the night before. At least he had some time to sleep and though he slept soundly enough, he dreamed uneasily about the Magi, who were in obvious danger, trekking across vast areas of desert and desolate wastelands. Nevertheless, he awoke fairly rested and went to his post at the appointed time. The wondrous star still shed its great light and Ethan could see everywhere as if it were daylight.

Then, just like the night before, around 3:00, the Roman third watch, there appeared several figures coming over the ridge above him. Unlike the previous night, these were not mounted on horses or camels. The few who were riding were on donkeys. The others were walking.

As they came closer, Ethan could distinguish the riders from those on foot and saw that the ones on the donkeys were women and those walking were men. It was a small group, no more than ten. "Dangerous," he thought. Even worse, he noticed that only a few of the men were armed. The party stopped several feet away. One of the men saluted as he approached and greeted Ethan in cordial Hebrew fashion.

Promptly returning the salute and greeting, Ethan asked, "Sir, are you lost?" Then he added, "This is not an area that is usually traveled at this time of night. Mostly, there are only hills and pastures for sheep or goats and cattle."

"We know," replied the man, "But we need help. We need to find a way to the road to Egypt without being discovered. Someone, very evil and powerful, seeks us. He wishes to kill our child. We understand that you shepherds know such a way."

Ethan was astounded. How was it, he thought, that just the night before the Magi had sought his help in finding another way and now here was this group? Surely this was more of God's work. That was all it could be. As on the previous night he felt he must help.

Though it also meant leaving his post again, Evan responded, "Yes, good sir, I know of such a way, but it is difficult and a misstep could lead to death."

"The difficulty will not bother us," the man replied. "God will protect us. Just show us the way."

"I will," Ethan said, "But you must follow me closely and do as I say."

"We will do whatever you direct. Now, let me tell the others." The man turned and went back to his group. In a few minutes he returned.

"We are ready," he said, "and we'll follow you. But first tell me your name."

Ethan told him his name and the man said, "I am Joseph." With a sweeping gesture of his arm he directed Ethan's attention to a woman in the front of the group, who was mounted on one of the donkeys and holding a baby. Proudly, he introduced them, "This is my wife, Mary, and our son, Jesus."

Ethan's heart stopped. "Oh, I should have known," he thought. "It is certainly God's plan for me to have been here last night and to be here tonight." It took a few seconds for him to recover his composure, but when he did, he went immediately to where Mary and the baby Jesus were. In all of his thirteen years, Ethan's experience with newborns had been mostly with lambs, but in seeing this child he had no doubt there had never been and never would be another one comparable to the baby Jesus. Like all the others who had seen him, Ethan marveled at such beauty and perfection, manifested so clearly in this one small child. With difficulty he turned away.

He took a deep breath and said to Joseph, "Follow me."

It was a different path from the one the Magi had taken but no less severe. Again with the aid of the star's great light they made it without mishap. At the top of the ridge, they stopped, and Joseph, as Malthus had done, knelt with Ethan in prayer. Ethan noticed that except for the women who remained on their donkeys, the other men knelt with them. Joseph praised God for His deliverance of them, for His goodness and grace and thanked Him for sending Ethan to help them. He too asked God's blessing upon Ethan and his family.

When they finished praying, they stood up and again, like Malthus, Joseph offered him some coins. Ethan thanked him but would not take them. For a reason he could not explain, it just didn't seem right. He told Joseph his blessing was sufficient. For another reason he couldn't explain he asked that Joseph continue to pray for him.

Joseph assured him he would. Just as he was about to ask Ethan not to tell anyone about them, Ethan told him not to worry, he would not divulge to anyone what had happened. And to Joseph's obvious bewilderment, he added, "Not even to my father."

They made their farewells, and Ethan watched them proceed slowly, but surely, down the sharp decline. Ethan did not hasten to return as he had the night before and although he derived great satisfaction from what he had done, for some reason he felt a foreboding, a profound sadness.

8

Eventually, things returned pretty much to normal in the lives of the shepherds. In a few days the star went away, just as the angels had. But the experiences of the shepherds on that cold winter night arose frequently in their thoughts and were the topic of many conversations among them for the remainder of their lives.

Ethan's father celebrated the glorious event, as he termed it, on the same day and night of each ensuing year until he died. Often he expressed regret that Ethan never saw the Christ Child and *always* he referred to Jesus as the "Christ Child." He firmly believed the child he saw was the Christ, the Saviour who had been foretold through all the prophecies and scripture. Although he also knew he would not live to see Him come into His kingdom, his hope was all he needed. While it was neither proof of anything nor even logical, it had been sufficient to change his life and assured him beyond any doubt that tomorrow's world would be better.

Not until Abel was dying did Ethan tell him about the Magi and the help he rendered to Joseph and Mary and the baby, Jesus. He even showed Abel the coins. To Ethan's welcome surprise, Abel was obviously pleased and relieved. He assured Ethan he understood why it was necessary to keep what he'd done a secret and how truly glad he was that Ethan had seen Jesus. With this knowledge, the guilt he had felt for depriving Ethan of seeing the Christ Child vanished. He died in peace, his face reposed with that same smile of contentment he had worn ever since that "glorious" night when he had seen Jesus and his life was transformed.

After Abel's death there was really no reason not to use the coins, but Ethan did not need to use them. More importantly, keeping the coins was absolute proof of what had happened and a reminder of why it had happened. For this reason they meant much more to him than anything they could buy and were far more valuable as an honored keepsake.

Long before Abel died, Ethan assumed full responsibility for the large flocks of sheep and the additional herds of goats and cattle that he and his father had acquired over the years. Ethan thanked God daily for his many blessings, often thinking of that holy night and the Magi and Joseph and Mary and Jesus. He wondered if he would ever see any of them again. As the years passed, he knew that the Magi were long past old age and probably dead, but Joseph and Mary and certainly Jesus, could easily be alive. Jesus would still be a young man.

Ethan, like his father, remained hopeful, and on the same day each year, he too, celebrated the night the star appeared and the nights he had spent with the Magi and Joseph, Mary and the baby Jesus. Ethan kept the three coins in a small, beautifully carved box and polished them frequently.

On the day each year when he commemorated the appearance of the great star and the angels and those wonderful events that followed, he gathered his family about him and told the story of the coins and how he helped Joseph, Mary and their baby, Jesus. No one, including Ethan, doubted in the least that the coins were Ethan's most valued possession and a positive symbol of his hope and faith in the coming Messiah.

9

Thirty years passed. Ethan was forty-three years old. His hair was gray, but he was still hearty and strong, as robust as many much younger men. One morning in early summer, when the grass grew green and lush, he stood on a familiar hillside watching a large flock of sheep that had once belonged to him grazing in the pasture below. Although they were no longer his, the sight still brought great pleasure to him. As his father had done for him, he had given his cattle and sheep to his son, who with his hired hands was now fully capable of caring for them. Ethan simply enjoyed being outside and reflecting upon his blessings and the goodness of God in his life.

The loss of his wife three years before had not lessened his faith. Although he missed her greatly, he was thankful for their lives together and for the fine son she had given him. Unlike many he knew, he believed as King David did, that at his death he would be with her again. As it was for King David, this assurance was his greatest comfort. Why others did not believe this Ethan did not know. Since his wife's death he often recalled what King David had said when his infant son died.

> While the child was still alive, I fasted and wept. I thought, 'Who knows? The Lord may be gracious to me and let the child live.'
> But now that he is dead, why should I fast? Can I bring him back again? *I will go to him, but he will not return to me.*

On this particular day he was roused from his thoughts by a crowd of people gathering at the base of a large hill some distance away. As he watched, the crowd grew quickly, transforming the hillside with its vast assortment of colors into a spectacular panorama. In a short time it numbered in the thousands. Ethan noticed too, that almost all the people, seated on the grass, were facing down the gentle slope. With his curiosity aroused he wanted a closer look and began to walk rapidly in that direction.

He arrived at the back of the crowd within minutes. While he caught his breath, he saw that everyone was listening to a strikingly handsome younger man seated on a rock in front of them

Ethan also began listening and was surprised he could hear so clearly from such a distance. There was something special about the speaker's voice. As he listened, the words and their messages touched him as nothing else he had ever heard. He wanted to hear more. What did the young man mean when he said, "I am the way and the truth and the life. No one comes to the Father except through me"? Certainly, the Father he referred to was God, but how could this man claim that the only way to reach God was through him? How could that be? Who was this man? Uncertainty clouded his thoughts.

Finally the young man ended his speaking and began to walk freely among the people talking to them, smiling at them, and touching many who reached out to him. Ethan had noticed a man standing next to him listening intently to everything the speaker had said. The man appeared to be as old or older than Ethan. Speaking to him, Ethan asked, "Sir, could you tell me the name of the young man who speaks so eloquently?"

"Certainly," the man replied. "His name is Jesus." Ethan's astonishment was obviously mistaken by the other man, who exclaimed, "Sir, are you all right? You look ill. Perhaps you should sit down."

"No--no," Ethan stammered, "I'm fine. I'm all right." After a few moments he did appear all right, but in his mind there remained troubling, unanswered questions.

Ethan talked further with the other man and learned that his name was Simon, a close follower of Jesus. That day Ethan also became a follower of Jesus. At least he became a follower in the sense that he followed Jesus almost everywhere he went and listened to him with utmost attention and respect. From time to time he gave Simon money to help with Jesus' expenses, but this was the extent of his involvement. He remained unsure about the kingdom Jesus intended to form and was totally at a loss about how he was going to save the Jews or anyone else. Still, he continued to listen to him and witnessed his healing the sick and performing many other miracles. He knew Jesus was sent by God as part of the plan for His Kingdom, but how was that plan to be accomplished? He just did not know. Although this question, as well as others he had, was not answered--or at least he did not think they were--Jesus taught many things he had never thought about.

10

On a day in late summer Jesus was visiting in a home near the Sea of Galilee and early in the morning he went down to sit by the seaside. The day, though warm, was not uncomfortable and overall was very pleasant. The sea itself was extraordinarily beautiful. A fine mist lay upon the calm blue water, glistening diamond like in the bright sunlight.

As it usually happened, a large number of people, including Ethan, had followed Jesus, and when he arrived at the shore, they pressed so closely about him he was unable to sit down. Nearby was a small boat anchored in the shallow water, and he waded out and sat in it. The people were so eager to hear him they remained standing on the shore while he talked to them from the boat.

Jesus' teaching was different from any other they had heard. John the Baptist attracted huge crowds with his dynamic preaching. His sermons were so forceful, so condemning and demanding that they caused many who heard them to be fearful and repent. Even though Jesus also taught repentance, he proclaimed it should be more a consequence of loving God than fearing Him.

His knowledge of the scriptures surpassed even that of the scribes, and his explanations made far more sense than theirs. What really drew people to Jesus were his stories; parables he called them. They all related to their everyday lives, their homes, personal relationships, work, crops, the sea and rivers, birds, fish, trees and other animals and things with which they were familiar. Jesus' favorite animals were sheep, which he often used to describe the people themselves, representing himself to them as their shepherd.

The parables were not just stories. They were lessons about God and His love, love of each other, right and wrong, heaven and hell, sin and salvation, faith, hypocrisy and much, much more. Some they knew had profound spiritual meanings and had they fully understood them they would have realized they all did. They would learn later this was just what Jesus intended, for instead of being discouraged by their lack of understanding, they were encouraged, stimulated to think more about what he told them. At the proper time understanding would come.

Jesus talked frequently about those in high places, the rich and powerful, denouncing them for their abuse of authority and their oppression of the poor and weak. It was amazing how much Jesus knew about such things. Even more remarkable, he spoke as though his authority was greater than theirs and he was not afraid to say so. He declared that his authority came directly from God, whom he often referred to as his father. This claim and his open defiance of such abuse only angered those who inflicted it and caused them to think of ways to silence him. At first, they tried to discredit him in open debate, and, failing miserably in their attempts, they hated him even more and sought other means to suppress him and his teaching. Ethan feared for Jesus' safety, but he shrugged it off, believing Jesus was too popular with the people for anyone to harm him. Besides, even those closest to him did not seem concerned. Closer to him than anyone else were twelve men, known as apostles, whom he had specifically selected to work with him. At times they would ask Jesus the meaning of a particular parable and he would explain it to them.

Jesus told many parables that day, and when it grew late, he gave the people his blessing and sent them to their homes. A good number, instead of going to their homes, followed him and his apostles to the house where he was staying and as many as could went inside with him. Others gathered outside at the open windows. Ethan was among those who went to the house and into the large room where Jesus and the apostles had gone. There the apostles asked him to explain a parable he'd told earlier that day and he did, making it so plain they wondered how they had failed to understand it.

Afterwards, without considering how weary Jesus might be, the others begged to hear more and out of compassion for them he consented to their pleas and continued conversing with them in parables into the early part of the night. Only then, after he had blessed them again and dismissed them, did they depart for their homes.

On that evening Jesus told two parables which Ethan did not understand, but for some reason he believed they held a special meaning for him. He was moved so deeply he committed the parables to memory and during the next several days repeated them over and over in his mind, hearing clearly the voice of Jesus as he had told them:

> Again, the kingdom of heaven is like unto a treasure hid in a field; the which when a man hath found, he hideth, and for joy thereof goeth and selleth all that he hath, and buyeth that field.
>
> Again, the kingdom of heaven is like unto a merchant man, seeking goodly pearls; who when he had found one pearl of great price, went and sold all that he had, and bought it.

Ethan struggled unsuccessfully for days trying to understand these parables. He believed both had the same meaning, simply expressed in two different ways, but this was no help in deciphering them. Although he was in a constant quandary thinking about the parables, he refused to give up.

11

Then, one day, without any particular thought or reason, the answer came to him, as though he had suddenly emerged from the darkest night into the brightest day. That it happened so quickly strengthened his belief that he was right. The more he thought about it the more certain he was.

Nothing was as valuable as a place in God's kingdom. Jesus called it the kingdom of heaven. By Ethan's interpretation, the meaning of these parables was that for a price a person could purchase such a place. Though it would be costly, the cost would not be the same for everyone.

Part of the puzzle was how these parables would apply to him. When he understood their meaning this part was also revealed. He was convinced it was what had happened over thirty years before with the Magi and the baby Jesus and the gift of the three coins. Now it was obvious to him that had been God's plan all along. He was to use the coins in some way to purchase his share of God's kingdom. They were like the treasure in the field and the pearl of great price. The coins had always been his most cherished possession, worth far more than anything else he had ever owned and up until now he had never considered parting with them. In fact, he owned nothing else except what it took to meet his basic needs and a little extra, having given the rest of his wealth to his son.

Ethan's next decision was that Jesus would have to be the one to determine what must be paid. For him, he believed in some way it would be the three coins. He had never spoken to Jesus directly. There were always the sick and infirm who surrounded Jesus wherever he was, and Ethan, truly believing their need was greater than his, never did any more than just listen from the edge of the crowd and observe.

Even now, when he thought it was something very important, he believed it would be wrong to push his way through all those miserable, sad, suffering people just to ask a question. After much thought he decided he would consult Simon and ask him what he should do.

Feeling immense relief with his decision, Ethan hurried to Simon's home in Capernaum. There Simon's mother told him that Simon had gone with Jesus and the other apostles and disciples to Jerusalem for the Passover. More than just disappointing, her information was quite alarming. Not only did it mean he could not see Simon, it renewed his concern for Jesus. He recalled too well what had happened just a few weeks before.

On a nearby mountain in the vicinity of Bethsaida Jesus fed well over five thousand people with what a young boy brought that day for his dinner: five small loaves of bread and two small fish. The day afterward, many who had eaten the bread and fish followed Jesus back across the sea to Capernaum. For a reason Ethan did not know they wanted Jesus to do something greater than what he had done the day before. They even asked for a sign that would convince them he was who he claimed to be. They naively recited scripture to him about what Moses had done:

> Our fathers did eat manna in the desert; as it is written, Moses gave them bread from heaven to eat.

No one denied that feeding more than five thousand people was a great miracle, but it only fed them for one day. Moses' miracle fed an entire nation for forty years.

Jesus replied that it was not Moses who provided the manna, but God. Not only did God give manna to sustain their ancestors in the wilderness, He now offered His people another kind of bread, a bread that would give them eternal life.

On hearing this, the people begged that he give some of this marvelous bread to them. To their persistent pleading, Jesus responded, saying:

> Your fathers did eat manna in the wilderness and are dead.
> This is the bread which cometh down from heaven, that a man may eat thereof, and not die. I am the living bread which came down from heaven; if any man eat of

this bread, he shall live forever; and the bread that I will give is my flesh, which I will give for the life of the world.

Most of those who heard him were only confused, but some Pharisees standing nearby were not the least bit confused. They declared quite bitterly that the words spoken by Jesus were blasphemous. Their conversation, which Ethan overheard, is what caused his concern.

Having been humiliated so many times in their debates with Jesus, the Pharisees were already angry. Then hearing him say he had come down from heaven as the bread of life really infuriated them. They vehemently agreed that he should be killed for his blasphemy and further agreed how this would be done.

Because of his popular following in Galilee they decided they must wait until he went into Judea, to Jerusalem. There he would be brought before the Sanhedrin, charged with blasphemy, tried, convicted and put to death. To them it was quite simple. The Pharisees knew how easy it would be to hire witnesses who could guarantee Jesus' conviction. The trial would be only a formality.

After hearing these things, Ethan went immediately to Simon and told him what he had heard. Simon assured him that Jesus was in no danger. Jesus, he said, was fully aware of the Pharisees' plot and to foil their plans he would not go to Jerusalem or even into Judea. Ethan was much relieved to hear this. Now, however, Jesus had gone to Jerusalem and Ethan was once more frightened for him.

12

There was no question that he must also go to Jerusalem. What he would do there he did not know, but he had to go. As quickly as possible, he prepared to travel.

Over the years, he and his flocks moved from time to time throughout Palestine, seeking new sources of water and richer pastures. When this was no longer necessary, he made his home in Galilee and from there he would travel to Jerusalem. Covering twenty to twenty-five miles a day it would still require four or five days to reach Jerusalem.

The thought of returning to Jerusalem for Passover brought back many wonderful memories. He had gone with his parents when he was a child and had taken his family several times during his son's childhood. Always it had been the most memorable time of the year.

Passover was primarily a commemoration of God's deliverance of the Hebrews from their bondage in Egypt fifteen hundred years before. It was a time of worship and thanksgiving, rededication and sacrifice. For both the individual and the nation it was a time of spiritual cleansing and healing. While it was, first and foremost, a sacred ceremony and a celebration of Jewish faith, it was much more.

Those going to Jerusalem to observe Passover were known as Pilgrims and for weeks in advance, hundreds of thousands moved in steady streams along the paths and roadways leading to the Holy City. Many of these would not be Jews, yet like the Magi, they recognized Yahweh, the Jehovah God of the Hebrews as the one true God, and came to worship Him at the Jewish Temple. These Pilgrims came from all parts of Palestine and from other lands and countries as well, often traveling great distances to join in this holy event.

Jewish law, following precepts of ancient Mosaic teaching, required every adult male to pay for the privilege of worshiping at the Temple with offerings of money and sacrifices. A list of acceptable offerings was compiled by the priests and posted upon the city gates. This list specified the nature and quantity of each offering, the purpose it served and whether it was mandatory or voluntary. Sacrifices of both animals and grain consisted of five principal kinds: burnt offerings, grain offerings, peace offerings, sin offerings and guilt offerings. Although the offerings provided indispensable funds for the operation and maintenance of the Temple, including the support of the priests, soldiers and temple workers, a greater and more meaningful purpose was that they supplied the life-blood of the worshipers' communion with God and their recognition of His absolute sovereignty and holiness.

Very few Pilgrims carried with them the grain and animals they would sacrifice. The burden of transportation and risk of loss was too great. Instead they sold their crops and animals at home and used the proceeds to buy what they needed in Jerusalem. As a result, the cost of everything in Jerusalem was severely inflated, a condition harshly felt by the Pilgrims but highly favored by the local merchants and farmers. Since Ethan did not intend to participate in the Temple ceremonies or in any of the non-religious festivities and activities, such a condition would affect him very little.

Nonetheless, it would be necessary that he join with others in making the journey. Even though there would be an almost unbroken caravan the entire way, it was always dangerous to travel alone. Too often, thieves and robbers, pretending to be Pilgrims, infiltrated the procession and robbed and stole from those who were least protected.

13

Two families, both of whom were Ethan's friends and neighbors, cordially invited him to go with them. He gladly accepted their invitation and was further pleased to learn they were leaving early the next morning.

Were he not so disturbed about Jesus and what he might find in Jerusalem, Ethan would have thoroughly enjoyed the pilgrimage. Walking was not too difficult and was made even easier by the distraction of joyful singing that filled the air everywhere up and down the endless line of travelers. The weather was perfect, mostly mild during the day and cool enough at night for fires to provide a welcome warmth.

What he enjoyed most of all were the children with their wide-eyed looks of gleeful anticipation and genuine pleasure. They were so carefree and happy. "There is no sound more beautiful," he thought, "than the laughter of children at play." For them it was a wonderful adventure, just as it had been for Ethan and his son at their age. Thinking of their loving trust and complete innocence reminded him of Jesus when some children were brought to him for his blessing. His disciples attempted to discourage the parents, saying Jesus should not be bothered. When Jesus saw what they were doing he was greatly displeased, and said to them:

> Suffer the little children to come unto me, and forbid
> them not, for of such is the kingdom of God

Then he took them in his arms, placed his hands on their heads and blessed them.

"Yes," Ethan thought, "That's exactly how the Kingdom of Heaven should be, filled with God's children, living in perpetual joy and excitement, free of all worries and cares forever."

14

About mid-morning of the fifth day Ethan and his companions arrived at the outskirts of Jerusalem. As in the past, when Ethan reached the top of the lower hill to the north and could see the magnificent walls of the city he felt an instant thrill. To some extent this feeling would normally remain for the entire Passover observance. Now that his mission had changed, the feeling would not last but would give way to his initial uneasiness and urgent need for haste.

The line of travelers stretching out ahead of Ethan did not proceed along the roadway to the gates of the city. Instead, the procession split into several segments with some going around the east side and others to the west. Ethan knew that his group would also follow to one side or the other. Only a relatively few of the Pilgrims could stay in Jerusalem. A city in which only about 80,000 normally resided could not possibly accommodate an overflow of perhaps a million. For this reason it was both a tradition and a necessity that the vast majority camp out in the hills overlooking Jerusalem and in the mornings come marching down the hillsides singing and praising God. As many as possible would come together at the Temple for the day's worship and sacrifices.

Having so much experience from past pilgrimages, Ethan and his group wasted little time in finding suitable places to camp. Without providing any details, Ethan said he needed to go into Jerusalem immediately and was not sure when he would return. The others received his announcement without comment or question. They simply wished him well and assured him they would watch over his few possessions while he was gone. Ethan told them how much he appreciated their kindness for inviting him and how much he had enjoyed their company and hospitality. He then proceeded down the path towards Jerusalem. Just before he moved out of sight he turned and waved to those still standing beside the trail above him. They waved in return and as he disappeared behind a large rock he heard their appeals for God to bless him. With a feeling of deep affection he thought, "Good friends are truly a rich, rich blessing."

15

The steep descent leveled out. His pace quickened and in only minutes he was moving with numerous others towards the eastern wall and its several gates that gave entry to the city. Ethan did not attempt to enter the city through any of the nearest gates but went to one further away that opened into the Lower City by the Pool of Siloam. It was not as congested here and he was able to pass through easily enough and begin to work his way back toward the Temple.

The streets and common areas were thronged with masses of people, jostling, shouting, laughing, singing and in general enjoying themselves, not seeming to mind being squeezed, pushed, shoved about and often going nowhere at all. The shops and markets were so crowded Ethan wondered how they could do any business. In addition, there were the temporary street vendors hawking their wares, falsely and shamelessly representing them to be the least expensive and of the highest quality. Ethan recalled that Zechariah had foreseen Jerusalem becoming so overrun with people and cattle that many would have to live outside the walls.

A great number of booths and stalls had been erected along the streets to house live animals and birds, which, ostensibly, were sold for sacrificial offerings. In truth, these creatures could seldom be used for that purpose because the law required they must be without blemish. Nothing less would be acceptable to the only One who is perfect. This meant that rarely did animals or birds bought in the common market place pass the close scrutiny of the Temple inspectors. Fortunately, only the most gullible bought with the expectation that the animals and birds they purchased could be used as sacrifices. Those more experienced bought for their own personal use and simply laughed contemptuously at the spurious claims of the merchants. With very few exceptions, only the animals and birds sold in the Temple were used in the sacrifices and as intended, the huge profits from such sales greatly enriched the Temple treasury. Ethan, because of his knowledge of animals, was wise enough to know there was not a sufficient number of unblemished animals to satisfy the sacrificial needs of so many people. He was also wise enough not to share his wisdom with anyone else.

16

Ethan made note of all the chaotic activity, but he was not distracted in the least from his primary purpose. As he moved through the crowds, he called out loudly and repeatedly the name of "Jesus" and whether anyone knew where he was. He was sure that it was because of Jesus' wide spread popularity that in no time at all a man called back that Jesus and his disciples had gone to Bethany. This response was confirmed by several other voices and Ethan breathed a long sigh of relief.

That Jesus had not been taken into custody and was not even in Jerusalem was exceptionally good news. He knew Bethany was only about two miles southeast of Jerusalem and less than an hour's walk, all downhill. The gate by which he had entered was the one nearest the road to Bethany. Turning in that direction his spirits lifted and his step became lighter.

It was known as the Jericho Road, wide, dusty, relatively smooth and well traveled, even in normal times. Now it was like all the other roadways, filled with more Pilgrims coming to Jerusalem, singing, laughing and praising God, just as it had been on the road from Galilee. As he was going in the opposite direction from the Pilgrims, who in places occupied the entire roadway, his progress was a little slower than he expected. However, they cheerfully stepped aside to let him pass, greeting him with words of blessing and good will. He laughed too, thanking them for their courtesy. Continuing in this manner made it seem that in no time at all he was in Bethany.

Along the way he recalled one of Jesus' parables, in which a Jewish man traveling alone from Jerusalem to Jericho was attacked by robbers who stripped him of everything he had, even his clothing, beat him severely and left him half dead beside the road. Jesus said that a priest happened to come along and saw the poor man lying there but ignored him and, crossing to the other side of the road, passed him by. Next a Levite, a Temple assistant, came by and did just as the priest had done. Then a Samaritan, whose people were despised by the Jews, came that way. Instead of going on, the Samaritan stopped and treated the man's wounds, carried him to an inn on his own donkey, rented a room and tended to him that night. The next day he paid the inn keeper and gave him an extra amount for the victim's care until he returned. Ethan recalled that Jesus had told this parable in response to a lawyer who asked him, "Who is my neighbor?"

Ethan believed he understood the parable and was satisfied that Jesus' explanation of "who is my neighbor" was quite clear. He also thought the parable was a concise description of the different kinds of people one encounters in life, and you can't tell which kind they might be by who they are. Ethan smiled, murmuring to himself, "There are those who beat you up, those who pass you up and those who help you up."

17

Once he entered town, he left the thoroughfare with all its congestion, and went into one of the wider side streets. Although it had been several years since he was last in Bethany, it did not appear to have changed. A few structures of sun-dried brick and stone stood square and clean on both sides of the street. Some of these were shops but most were dwellings. All were colorfully arrayed for Passover with displays of flowers in the windows and doorways and in baskets hanging here and there along the walls. In spite of Ethan's pressing concern, he noticed with delight the beauty and charm of the scene before him. No wonder Jesus would rather come to a place like this, he thought, than venture into the chaotic world of Jerusalem.

Ethan knew no one in Bethany. The times he had been there he was only passing through, and although Bethany was a small town, it was large enough for Ethan to need directions. He saw several people coming towards him. As they approached he greeted them and asked if they knew Jesus. Eagerly, they all said they did. He then asked if they knew where he could find him. One of them, a young man, replied, "Jesus and his disciples are guests of Simon the Leper. Of course, he doesn't have leprosy any more. Jesus healed him about a year ago. But he's still called 'Simon the Leper' and doesn't seem to mind it. If I was as rich as he is I wouldn't care what people called me either. Anyway, his house is the really big one just beyond that long bend in the road." The young man turned as he spoke and pointed back in the direction from which they had come. Ethan thanked him and said to all of them, "Go with God and His blessings." They responded, almost in unison, "And God be with you as well."

Smiling, he moved quickly past them and headed towards the bend in the road, about two hundred yards or, at most, a furlong away. In just minutes he could see the house, which was indeed large, surrounded by a high wall with a massive wrought iron gate in front. Seconds later he was standing before the gate, and on the other side was a sight Ethan could never have imagined. A huge court yard, an atrium, lay before him, inlaid with beautiful mosaic tiles of many colors and designs, bordered with palms, small shade trees, and flowering plants. In its center was a fountain with water spouting several feet in the air, then falling in a glistening cascade into a large ornate basin surrounding it. Ethan would have further marveled had he known that the water came from a reservoir on top of the house, which was filled by infrequent rains and hand drawn water from deep wells outside the walls. Much more than an attraction, the fountain provided all the water used by Simon the Leper's household.

With continuing amazement Ethan closely noted the house and its surroundings. Built in the shape of the Hebrew letter *cheth,* it had two floors with covered porches extending along the fronts of its three sides. A large number of people were present, some standing in small groups, obviously engaged in conversation. Others were moving about on both the upper and lower porches. A good number were servants, laden with large platters, dishes and bowls. The platters and dishes he could see were heaped with various kinds of food, huge cuts of meat, whole birds and fish, as well as vegetables, fruits and breads. There were also servants carrying flagons and larger jugs, *askoses*, which Ethan was sure contained wine. On the lower porches and along the edges of the courtyard, men reclined in Roman fashion on couches and divans eating from the plates of food and drinking from the cups placed next to them on low square tables.

While Ethan was deciding what he should do, one of the men rose from a couch and came towards him. As he approached, Ethan saw that it was Simon, smiling and waving. Ethan smiled and waved in return. When Simon was closer, he said, "Ethan, I am so glad to see you. We're having a wonderful time. It's so good you can join us."

Ethan replied, "It's good to see you too, Simon. I pray you are well."

"We are indeed, Ethan, but I am no longer known as 'Simon.' Now I am 'Peter.' He laughed lightly, "Jesus changed my name. He said something about me being a rock. I don't really know what he meant, but if that is what he wants to call me, that's fine with me. However, this place does belong to a 'Simon.' He's known as Simon the Leper. Even though he doesn't have leprosy now, he's still called that. Doesn't seem to mind. Really too rich to mind anything. But Jesus healed him over a year ago and, as you can imagine, Jesus is the center of his life, and today of course, he's the guest of honor. Come on in and I'll introduce you to Simon. Jesus hasn't come out yet." With that Peter opened the gate and Ethan stepped through.

No longer concerned about Jesus' safety, Ethan's thoughts turned to his dilemma about the coins. He decided he would consult Peter as he originally intended, but he did wonder why Simon or rather "Peter" did not ask him why he was there. Perhaps Peter hadn't thought about it or it just didn't make any difference to him. He would assume the latter since Peter wasn't one to meddle. When he had the chance, he'd talk to him.

18

They walked toward a group of men standing in front of the center porch. Ethan could hear them laughing. A large man, also laughing, with a long gray beard and heavy gold chains hanging loosely down the front of his brightly colored robe stepped away from the others and came to meet them. Smiling broadly he extended his hand to Ethan.

Peter said, "Simon, this is my good friend, Ethan, from Galilee."

As Ethan took Simon's hand, Simon said, "Welcome, Ethan, I am Simon." He chuckled. "Better known as 'Simon the Leper,' but thanks to the Lord Jesus it should be 'Simon the Ex Leper.' However, I do not object to being reminded of my former uncleanness and the wonderful cleansing and healing of me by my dear Lord. I am so glad you came. There is ample food and refreshment, I believe." He chuckled again. "I place you in Peter's capable hands. He can show you where to clean up and find you a suitable place to partake of my humble fare." Laughing, he added, "Anything you want, dear friend, please just ask. But I do need to speak to my other guests, so please excuse me. Enjoy yourself!" With that he turned and walked away before Ethan could even thank him.

After Ethan had bathed, he rejoined Peter and walked with him to the porch on the other side of the courtyard. On the porch couches in no particular order were arranged in what the Romans called *trichinia*. A *trichinium* was a set of three couches, with two placed about seven feet apart parallel to each other and both perpendicular to the third. Dishes of food, a small flagon and cup rested on the small table placed conveniently by each couch. They stopped at the one where Peter had been when Ethan was at the gate. Its three couches were unoccupied. Pointing to one, Peter said, "Make yourself comfortable, Ethan, and enjoy some of this delicious food and wine. You won't find any better, anywhere."

"Thank you," Ethan replied.

Lying down, he did not realize how tired he was until he stretched out on the thick cushions and leaned back into the big, soft pillows. Following Peter's example he poured wine into a cup and drank. Just as Peter said, it was the best he'd ever had. He took another sip and slowly swallowed, fully savoring its fine flavor. He had heard the story about Jesus' first miracle, when he turned water into wine at a wedding in Cana and how the host had commented about how good it was, being so much better than any other they'd had. Ethan knew Peter was with Jesus when he performed the miracle. In a joking manner he laughedand said, "Simon must get Jesus to make his wine."

Peter smiled and replied, "You might not believe it, but if he had, you'd be drinking even better wine than this."

"That *is* unbelievable," Ethan exclaimed, "but I'll certainly take your word for it."

"Good," said Peter, "Let's eat."

With the first taste Ethan knew Peter was also right about the food. In just minutes he had consumed more than enough to satisfy his hunger. For some reason, he recalled the night he guided the Magi over the mountain and how hungry he was when he returned to the camp. A different time and situation, he thought, yet the food is the only real difference between then and now. Even though he thoroughly enjoyed what he'd just eaten, it did no more to satisfy him than the bread and cheese had. As he further reflected, he thought about what Jesus said after he fed those thousands in Bethsaida. Ethan realized it wasn't physical hunger Jesus was talking about, but spiritual, and that in some way he could satisfy *that* hunger---forever. He just wondered why Jesus didn't say how he would do it."

19

Having eaten, Ethan's attention shifted to the middle of the center porch, where Simon was lying upon an extra-large couch surrounded by several oversized pillows that blended so well with his robe he was almost invisible. Ethan noticed a handsome young man reclining upon an equally large couch to the left of Simon's. They were both laughing. What was so remarkable was how happy they looked. He said to Peter, "I know Simon has every reason to be happy, but that young man with him looks just as happy, if not more so."

Peter laughed, "I guess he does. Jesus healed Simon, but that young man had died and Jesus brought him back to life. His name is Lazarus. You see that large table over there where the servants are getting platters and bowls of food to serve?"

Ethan said he did. Peter continued, "You see those two lovely young women, who are directing the servants and putting the food out for them to serve?"

Ethan replied, "I sure do," and laughed.

"Well," Peter said, "they're his sisters, Mary and Martha. Their family is very rich and all three are perhaps Jesus' dearest friends. I know he loves them, and they, of course, love him dearly. He usually stays with them when he is in Bethany, but Simon insisted it was his turn and they consented on the condition he would let them help.

"Anyway, it was not long ago we had gone over Jordan to Perea, where Jesus ministered to the people there, teaching them and healing the sick. We had been in Jerusalem, but we left when some crazy people tried to stone him. They were probably hired by the Pharisees, who, as you know, hate him. So we were there in Perea when the message came that Lazarus was sick. Because of what happened in Jerusalem, we didn't think it wise to come back, and when two days had passed, we assumed he agreed. Then he announced he needed to come back, that Lazarus was dead. He said something very strange, so strange that I remember it clearly:

> This sickness is not unto death, but for the glory of
> God, that the Son of God might be glorified thereby.

Naturally, none of us thought it was safe. Of course, that didn't matter to me. I'll follow Jesus wherever he goes, and I'll say this for Thomas. He spoke very strongly in favor of coming back if that was what Jesus wanted. So we came back.

As you might expect, when we arrived, we were told Lazarus was dead. Somehow Jesus already knew. When he told us that in Perea, we decided then that was the reason he didn't hurry. If Lazarus was dead nothing could be done." Peter chuckled, "So we thought." He paused.

"Go on," Ethan said. "What happened next?"

Peter continued, "Well, the next is what you're not going to believe. Someone had gone ahead and told Martha and Mary that Jesus was coming, and before we had gotten into town, Martha ran out to meet us. She was heartbroken but awfully glad to see Jesus. We all felt so sorry for her. She said she knew that if he had been there, he would have healed Lazarus and even then she knew that God would give him whatever he asked. Jesus said something about Lazarus rising again and about the resurrection and quite a bit more, but I won't go into all that. I remember what he said, but I'm not sure I understand what he meant. Martha was confused too, and she simply said she knew he was the Christ, the Son of God and she left.

"For some reason we stayed where we were and it wasn't long before Mary was there. She seemed more upset than Martha. She fell down at Jesus' feet, crying, and said exactly what Martha had said about knowing that if Jesus had been there he would have saved Lazarus. Jesus didn't say as much to her as he had to Martha. I'm sure it was because she and those with her were so distraught. They were all in tears. Jesus felt so sorry for them he wept too. He just asked where Lazarus was buried and they led us to his tomb.

"Being as wealthy as they were, the tomb was huge. It was cut into the rock with a big stone set over the entrance." Peter took a deep breath. "This is where it really becomes unbelievable." He paused again.

"Please, go on," Ethan urged.

"Well," Peter continued, "Jesus asked for the stone to be removed. You can only imagine how shocked we were. Even Martha, who never questioned him, protested, saying, 'Lord, by this time he stinketh, for he hath been *dead* four days.'

"As reassuringly as possible, Jesus replied very softly, 'Said I not unto thee, that, if thou wouldest believe, thou shouldest see the glory of God?'

"When he said that, Martha directed the servants to push the stone aside. I can't tell you how scared I was, and I believe everyone else was too. I don't know of what, but standing there looking into the darkness of that tomb just sent a chill over me. Then Jesus raised his eyes toward heaven and prayed:

> Father, I thank thee that thou hast heard me.
> And I knew that thou hearest me always,
> but because of the people which stand by
> I said it, that they may believe that thou
> hast sent me.

After he prayed, he immediately stepped closer to the opening and cried in a loud voice,

LAZARUS, COME FORTH!

"I tell you, Ethan, I began trembling so much I almost collapsed. Two or three of the women did faint and several others, men and women, turned and ran away.

"What happened then was absolutely terrifying. Lazarus came hobbling out of that tomb into the daylight with his feet bound, grave clothes hanging off him and the napkin still around his face. It was truly a frightening, ghastly sight, but when Jesus instructed the servants to loose him and let him go, they did, though they were shaking so much it was very difficult. This, I must say was understandable, as they were really no more frightened than anyone else.

"Someone did have the forethought to hand them a robe to cover Lazarus, and once that was done, Lazarus appeared as though nothing had happened. What moments before had been such a painful, grief-filled experience, suddenly turned into one of exuberant thanksgiving and joy.

"Mary and Martha, as you would expect, rushed upon Lazarus instantly, embracing him with such lavish, loving affection--kisses, caresses, all that. We were all laughing, shouting praises and jumping around like crazy people. It was indeed 'a time to dance' and praise God. Words are just not adequate to describe our emotions.

"Finally, we were literally worn out and Martha and Mary went to where Jesus was standing. Kneeling at his feet, they thanked him over and over again and shed many more tears. Only this time they wept tears of joy. Jesus said nothing; simply smiled at them with the kindest, most tender expression I have ever seen.

"Lazarus, you know, had no idea what had happened, but you can be assured, he heard all about it later. What a celebration we had. Remember the parable Jesus told about the unworthy son, who wasted his inheritance?"

"I certainly do," Ethan answered.

"Well," Peter went on, "I was reminded of that parable, the part about the banquet the father held, when his son returned home after so many years and the father thought he was dead. As Jesus said in the parable, 'they began to make merry.' And that is exactly what we did, in a very big way.

"Then there's the part when the father spoke to the other son and told him:

> It was meet that we should make merry, and be glad;
> for this thy brother was dead, and is alive again; and was
> lost, and is found.

Of course, Lazarus was not unworthy and did not waste an inheritance, but he was a brother who was dead and miraculously brought back to life. I can think of no greater cause for merriment and celebration."

"Neither can I!" Ethan exclaimed. With equal fervor he added, "What an extraordinary, wonderful, beautiful story. And to think, you witnessed it all. What a privilege! What a blessing!"

"Yes, it was," Peter replied. "Now you know why Lazarus looks so happy. It was all so absolutely fantastic.

"But you know, Ethan, there's something else I've thought about. The parable Jesus told about the rich man and the poor man who was also named Lazarus. You remember that one?"

"I do," said Ethan.

"Well, think about this. Both died. The rich man went to hell; the poor man to Father Abraham's bosom. The rich man, you recall, asked Father Abraham to send Lazarus back to his father's house and witness to the rich man's brothers; thinking that if they heard the truth from someone who came back from the dead they'd believe him and repent. Now, I think Jesus gave Lazarus that name in the parable knowing he was going to bring someone named Lazarus back from the dead. *And,* we know that he did just that, and what was the unbelievers' reaction? When the unbelieving Pharisees learned that Lazarus was alive did they become believers and repent? Not at all. In fact, because it was Jesus who restored Lazarus to life, they hated Jesus so much they sought to kill Lazarus, just to--I guess, nullify in some way what Jesus had done. After all, Lazarus was living proof of Jesus' power. But more to the point, do you recall Abraham's response to the rich man?"

Ethan replied, "'[I]f they hear not Moses and the prophets, neither will they be persuaded, though one rose from the dead.'" He thought for a moment, then exclaimed, "Oh, I see! I understand what you're saying. Just like the Egyptian Pharaoh, Jesus knew that the hearts of some people cannot be changed. Bringing Lazarus back to life was definite proof of that."

"*That* is correct," said Peter. "I really believe that's what Jesus was doing and I'm glad to hear you agree. Thank you."

20

While Ethan pondered what Peter had said, a servant appeared. He bowed to Ethan, "Sir, the Master wishes to see you."

Ethan asked, "Simon?"

"No sire," the servant responded, "The Lord Jesus."

Ethan was dumbfounded. How did Jesus know he was there? He didn't even know him. Why would he want to see him? He knew nothing about the coins. Had he done something wrong? Completely bewildered, his heart racing, he instinctively looked to where Simon was and saw Jesus, just as Peter had implied, reclining on the couch to Simon's right, the place of honor. Bewildered as he was, he noted that Lazarus was not there. Peter appeared as perplexed as Ethan, but nodded for him to go. Ethan rose slowly from the couch and followed the servant across the courtyard to Simon's *trichinium*. Ethan dared not look at Jesus, but kept his eyes fixed on Simon, who watched him approach, smiling warmly. When he drew within hearing, Simon sat upright and said, "Ethan, the Lord Jesus wishes to speak with you. Regrettably, I must ask you once more to excuse me. There's a matter that needs my attention." With that he placed his feet on the floor, stood up, bowed to Jesus, smiled again at Ethan and disappeared into the house.

Still reluctant to look at Jesus, but unable to resist, Ethan turned to him and in that moment his apprehension fled. Jesus was smiling--warm, friendly, reassuring--his eyes transfixing Ethan's with an intensity that banished all anxiety. He could not explain or even describe their effect on him. He only knew that when Jesus looked into his eyes, he was transformed and desired very much to hear what Jesus would say. Regardless of why Jesus had summoned him, he knew everything would be all right.

With both hands Jesus reached out to him and Ethan eagerly took them. Immediately, there came over him a feeling of elation--peaceful, comforting, absolute. Later, he would understand what Jesus meant by his invitation to those he called "sheep without a shepherd." How lovingly and tenderly he entreated them:

> Come unto me, all *ye* that labour and are heavy laden,
> And I will give you rest.
> Take my yoke upon you and learn of me;
> For I am meek and lowly in heart:
> And you shall find rest unto your souls.
> For my yoke is easy, and my burden is light.

In Jesus' gentle grasp, Ethan thought, "Could the 'yoke' be the loving embrace of his arms and the 'burden' his love itself?"

Jesus drew him to the foot of the couch where he could sit. There Jesus released his hands and spoke to him in the soft, soothing voice he so often and effectively used to provide comfort and dispel fear and doubt.

Afterward, Ethan could not recollect everything Jesus said; he was so enthralled just being in his presence, but he remembered vividly that Jesus knew all about him: his experiences with the Magi, the coins, his assistance in guiding Joseph and Mary, who was holding Jesus, over the mountain that cold winter night. In years to come he would remember clearly how Jesus' eyes twinkled and how easily he laughed as he recounted those events for him.

Even before Ethan could say anything, Jesus told him not to be concerned about the coins; when the time came, he would know what he should do with them. Ethan felt instantly relieved, but somehow sensed he should go. He slipped from the couch to his knees and fervently implored, "Your blessing, Master, please."

His eyes filled with compassion, Jesus placed his hands upon Ethan's head and once more Ethan felt the "rest unto his soul" he had known a few minutes before. The assurance that this feeling could and would last forever would come at another time. When Jesus had given his blessing, he again took Ethan's hands in his and lifted him to his feet.

Standing there before Jesus, his voice quivering and in barely more than a whisper, he murmured, "Thank you, Master. Thank you." Then, for a reason he could not explain he added almost tearfully, "Goodbye, my Lord."

21

As he returned to rejoin Peter, Ethan fought in vain for his mind to regain control of his feelings. Try as he could he was unable to. He could not comprehend what it was all about. There was no explanation for what had happened. That it was not anything he was supposed to explain or understand did not occur to him. Eventually it would become clear that his experience was not for instruction, but preparation. Jesus had reached not only into Ethan's heart, but had also touched his soul--something Ethan could not have known, though in time he would. Until then, all he knew was that he'd had the most marvelous experience of his life.

Peter could tell by Ethan's expression that Jesus had affected him deeply. But he would have been more than surprised if that had not happened. He knew from his own experiences how Jesus touched you in ways you could not understand. Although Peter had spoken lightly of Jesus' renaming him, the reason for this puzzled him constantly, and as of yet he had no answer.

Contrary to what most people do when they have an extraordinary experience, Ethan did not wish to share his with Peter. It was not like being cured of leprosy or even being raised from the dead. Those were external experiences to which anyone could relate, easy to describe, even to see. Trying to share the inexplicable and mysterious events in one's life might only lead to greater confusion and uncertainty.

Perhaps Peter understood this. In any event he was kind enough not to say anything. He simply poured a cup of wine and handed it to Ethan, who took it gratefully.

Just as Ethan emptied the cup and set it down, Peter pointed towards Simon's *trichinium* and exclaimed, "Would you look at what Mary's doing!"

Ethan looked and was as startled as Peter. Mary was standing over

Jesus, her beautiful, delicate features cast in a look of profound sadness. She held in her hand an alabaster jar, known to hold a Roman pound of genuine spikenard, a very costly perfume.

Everyone watched, fascinated, as she opened the jar and proceeded to anoint Jesus' head, slowly pouring upon it a portion of the precious nard. Then, with the utmost dignity, she moved to the foot of the couch and with the remainder of the ointment anointed Jesus' feet, the strong sweet fragrance rising and spreading over the entire courtyard.

When the jar was empty, Mary put it aside and to the utter disbelief of those present she removed her head band. Instantly, her lustrous black hair tumbled in thick shimmering folds upon her shoulders and down her back. The mood of several who were watching changed as quickly as the falling of her hair. Their casual curiosity turned abruptly to vocal disapproval; a reaction that became even more pronounced by what she did next.

Jewish custom strictly forbade women to expose their hair in public. Only those of loose morals did such things. Yet, having already violated this custom, Mary, in further defiance, stooped to cover Jesus' feet with her hair and in an obvious expression of worship wiped them with it.

Neither Ethan nor Peter joined in the protest. Ethan was too moved by the graphic beauty of the ritual even to consider that Mary was doing anything wrong, and Peter probably felt the same. Whatever their feelings, that which followed caused even greater dissension.

When Mary finished, she straightened up, her hair cascading in lovely loose waves about her body. Then, without even glancing at Jesus she gracefully walked away, having never said a word, still looking as though her heart would break.

On the porch nearby was a group of men, some of those who objected to Mary's anointing of Jesus. As she approached the group, one of them, an apostle whom Ethan recognized as Judas Iscariot, confronted her. In a loud, angry voice, he demanded, "Why was not this ointment sold for three hundred pence and given to the poor?" His companions voicing their agreement, murmured, "Why *was* the waste of this ointment made?"

Ethan had never liked Judas and wondered why he was the one entrusted to handle the finances for Jesus and the apostles. He had heard and seen enough to know that Judas was not interested in helping the poor.

He believed that had Mary turned the spikenard over to him he would have been the only one to profit from it.

Apparently, Jesus heard what had been said for he suddenly appeared and stepping between Mary and Judas, he severely rebuked Judas and his companions:

> Let her alone: against the day of my burying hath she kept this.
>
> She hath done what she could: she is come aforehand to anoint my body to the burying. For ye have the poor always with you always, and whensoever ye will ye may do them good; but me ye have not always.

Ethan was not exactly sure what Jesus meant, other than he was defending Mary, but he noticed they all became quiet, except for Judas, who, with his head lowered, stalked away, muttering to himself. Ethan watched him go straightway to the gate and opening it, turn and look back with the most hateful, malevolent scowl Ethan had ever seen.

All at once Ethan felt extremely uncomfortable. There was too much he did not understand. Being with Jesus had been unbelievably wonderful, but now with everything else that had happened he was all mixed up. The relief he felt when he learned Jesus was not in Jerusalem was gone, leaving him confused and disheartened. Mary's anointing of Jesus was a tender, beautifully moving tribute, something he would always remember. Still, in spite of its serene and peaceful appearance, there was an ominous air about it he could not shake off. Neither could he rid his mind of Judas' face, a mask of malice and anger, leering back at them from the gate. A heavy sense of foreboding came over him, just as it had the night, he'd led Joseph and Mary with Jesus up the mountain. For him this was not a time for feasting and making merry.

There was no doubt Judas was evil and intended to do Jesus harm. Sadly, Ethan had no idea what could be done about it. He just knew he could no longer remain in such festive surroundings and whether right or not, he felt strongly compelled to rejoin his friends--just as soon as he could.

22

Peter appeared very disappointed when Ethan told him he was leaving but was gracious enough not to ask why. Nevertheless, he did try to change his mind.

"You know," Peter said, "you're not going to find any better food anywhere else or as much of it."

Ethan agreed.

"Neither." continued Peter, "does anyone else have wine as fine as Simon's."

Again Ethan agreed.

Undeterred, Peter persisted, "What is even more important than the food and wine is that you will not have the benefit and pleasure of my company."

Ethan smiled and said, "I can't argue with anything you've said, Peter. I've enjoyed everything immensely, especially your company. You have been a dear friend, but I feel I must go".

Although he had not actually enjoyed everything, he knew if he mentioned Judas there was no telling when he could get away. He then embraced Peter and stepping back, said with utmost sincerity, "God be with you."

"With you also," Peter replied as Ethan turned and walked away.

When he found Simon and thanked him for his hospitality Simon seemed as disappointed as Peter that he was not staying. Expressing concern about how late it was and since he had no where to go, Simon insisted Ethan spend the night. Ethan thanked him again and explained that he was camping with friends in the hills, where, he assured Simon, he would be quite comfortable. Though Simon doubted how comfortable he would be, he did not argue and sent Ethan on his way with his blessing.

Ethan looked for Jesus but failed to find him. He thought Jesus might have left because of the unpleasantness with Judas. Whatever the reason, Ethan was relieved. Feeling as he did, he was afraid that seeing him again would upset him even more.

23

It was a little over an hour before sunset and though traffic on the Jericho Road had diminished, the enthusiasm of those Pilgrims still on it had not. In spite of his low spirits, Ethan was quickly caught up in their exuberance and literally swept along by them to Jerusalem. From there it was just a relatively short climb to where his friends were camped.

Darkness had not yet fallen, but already the surrounding hillsides burgeoned with thousands of amber and reddish gold patches of blazing campfires and flaming torches. As a rule the torches marked only major paths and trails leading to the numerous camping areas. Ethan's path was not used much, and he had to laugh at the seeming violation of the rule when he saw torches marking his path. There was no doubt whom he should thank for this handiwork, and as soon as he saw them they would be.

As he climbed, he recalled those two nights when the Great Star, shining as brightly as another sun, illuminated his way. With his recollection came the inevitable awareness of the difference between the Star's overwhelming light and that of the torches. That difference clearly demonstrated the vast, incomparable difference between God's power and man's.

He then asked himself, "How or where does Jesus fit into all this?" He remembered Jesus saying he was the light of the world. There were times when his face shone with a bright radiant glow that was certainly brighter than the torches, but nothing like the Great Star. Slowly, he shook his head and wondered what it all meant.

24

Ethan entered the camp, just as the last rays of sunlight were disappearing below the upper line of trees on the Mount of Olives. With the setting of the sun, a light cool breeze arose, blowing gently into the trees, stirring and rippling their leaves so that the fading light flickered star like through the branches.

Warmed considerably from his climb, Ethan found the breeze refreshing, but he knew that once he stopped, without additional clothing or a fire, he would quickly become chilled.

With this in mind it was a welcome sight not only to see his friends, but to see them gathered comfortably about their fires. Needless to say they were also glad to see him and though the evening meal was over, food was immediately brought out and Ethan was urged to eat. Because of the feast he'd enjoyed at Simon's he wasn't really hungry, but out of courtesy and respect to his friends he accepted at least enough to ease any concern they might have for his hunger.

Had they known how well he had dined at Simon's, there would have been no thought of concern. Their urging, perhaps, was no more than simple courtesy or may have been due to the Passover rule that prohibited eating anything until after the morning Temple services. That meant nothing could be eaten until sometime after midday.

Fasting and experiencing the pangs of hunger were considered essential to proper worship. Ethan understood this and believed in the value of it, but he did not think that to properly worship God you should have to suffer. Surely God did not expect that. He knew that when King David and his men were obviously famished they ate the holy, consecrated bread in the tabernacle. Not only did the priest give his permission, but Jesus also approved of what they did.

Ethan recalled the Sabbath when Jesus and his disciples were going through a corn field and the disciples, being hungry, plucked some corn and ate it. The Pharisees, seeing them, claimed they were violating the law which forbade crops being harvested on the Sabbath. They then severely criticized Jesus, blaming him for his disciples' transgression.

Everyone knew that taking corn from someone else's field was not a violation of law. Scripture specifically allowed this practice, providing:

> When thou comest into the standing corn of thy neighbor, then Thou mayest pluck the ears with thine hand; but thou shalt not move a sickle unto thy neighbor's standing corn.

It did not say, "[T]hou mayest pluck the ears with thine hand; *except on the Sabbath.*" Using a sickle might be considered harvesting, but of course a sickle was not used. Ethan was confident Jesus knew this scripture, but in response to the Pharisees' rebuke he did not refer to it. He instead reminded them of what David had done and also told them, "The Sabbath was made for man, and not man for the Sabbath." Ethan found Jesus' answer especially appealing. Obviously, God meant for the observance of the Sabbath to be uplifting rather than oppressive, and, like all of Jesus' teaching, it just made good sense. Then for no apparent reason Jesus had added, "Therefore the Son of Man is Lord also of the Sabbath" and Ethan was not sure what that meant. He just knew there was nothing wrong with eating on the Sabbath. Preparing meals on the Sabbath was forbidden, as that involved labor, but the Sabbath was not a day of fasting and pulling an ear of corn from a stalk and eating it required no more labor than taking food from a dish and putting it in your mouth.

This interchange between Jesus and the Pharisees was not the first time Ethan had witnessed the intense hostility of the Pharisees toward Jesus. Their hatred was so great that distorting the interpretation of scripture to justify their feelings was more their rule than the exception.

Allowing himself to dwell on these thoughts only intensified his feelings of frustration and dire concern for Jesus. He wanted to share his apprehension with the others, but then he thought, why burden them? They were in such a jovial mood and would most likely not understand why he was disturbed. As he himself had often rationalized, it seemed impossible that someone as popular as Jesus, obviously a man of God, could be so despised that there would be those who desired to kill him. Even without knowing the details and as illogical as it seemed, Ethan felt the stark reality of the evil of which Judas and the Pharisees were capable.

25

With the evening prayers and the singing of hymns, Ethan's feeling of dread thankfully diminished. During this time of devotion and praise, the glory of God was lauded in every camp on every hillside. In exalting God's majestic sovereignty and infinite power and extolling His mighty works, one indisputable truth prevailed; a truth proclaimed with such passion and conviction that Ethan's fears were eased and moved him to humbly and fervently acknowledge God's sovereignty with his own imploring plea:

> O God, I know You have told us through King David
> that we are not to fret because of evil doers, 'for they shall
> be cut down like the grass, and wither as the green herb.'
> I know too, O God, that You are the only true God and
> all things are ordained and controlled by You and are
> subject to your will. I earnestly pray that You will comfort
> me, O God, in this truth, and that neither Judas nor the
> Pharisees and the evil they might do will ever triumph.

Throughout all the campgrounds vespers marked a reverent and peaceful close to the long day, and the Pilgrims prepared for a short night of rest as they unrolled their pallets and blankets and made the places they would sleep as comfortable as possible. For a fleeting moment Ethan thought of the plush comfort of the couch at Simon's, but having spent most nights of his adult life sleeping on the ground, it seemed only natural to be doing it now. He thought no more about anything other than his own preparations for the night.

26

Although not as upset as he had been, Ethan still had much on his mind, and only when he finally succumbed to the weariness of the day did he sleep. It seemed as though he had just lain down when he was suddenly awakened. The air was alive with happy voices raised in a varied mix of song and praise. Already fires were burning, casting their weak illumination into the early morning gloom.

Ethan sat up abruptly, letting the warm covering of his cloak and blanket slip to the firm pallet of straw that had been his bed. Freed of this warmth, he shivered slightly in the pre-dawn chill and quickly pulled the cloak about his shoulders. A few moments passed before he was fully awake, and then, just as it had been the night before, he was roused by the worshipful excitement of the joyful sounds around him. He remembered his prayer and the feeling of relief and comfort it brought. Today he would go with the others to worship at the Temple and renew his faith in Almighty God.

Ethan rose quickly, and to the cheerful greetings from the others he replied with equal enthusiasm, sincerely wishing them a blessed and glorious day. Feeling far more content than he had for days, he kept saying to himself, "God, the worries of life are ours, not Yours, but we can rely upon You to resolve them for us and give us Your grace and peace."

Ethan rolled his bedding and went to the place assigned to the men for their toiletries. Afterward, he joined the others as they gathered to make their descent to the Temple.

By then the sun had nudged out the grayness of dawn and fully emerged to shed its light upon the Pilgrims who streamed in colorful procession down the hillsides, voicing their adoration and reverence of God in joyous song and adulation.

Ethan and his friends merged easily with other Pilgrims as they made their way to the roads leading to the Temple. He listened enthralled, hearing the heartfelt strains of praise and worship fill the surrounding hills and valleys, sounding and resounding unbelievably in marvelous accord. It was, he thought, like the heavenly chorus of angels on the night of Jesus' birth. Though perhaps not as spectacular or as melodious as angels, the Pilgrims were also glorifying "God in the highest." Ethan felt truly thrilled and inspired to be a part of it.

27

As the serpentine lines poured down the hills and converged upon the roadways below, the crescendo continued, loud, joyful and reverent. Infused with all that he heard and felt, Ethan eagerly raised his voice with the others.

They had not gone far, when Ethan stopped singing and looked down in amazement at the scene before him. There he saw Jesus seated comfortably upon the back of a young colt, a foal of a donkey, heavily draped with several layers of men's garments. Ethan stared in wonder as he watched the donkey with Jesus moving in an unhurried, even solemn manner, along the main thoroughfare towards Jerusalem, the foal's mother trailing dutifully behind. Ethan looked with profound admiration at the regal bearing of Jesus, accentuated by the diminutive size of the colt. Turning neither right nor left, Jesus' eyes were obviously fixed solely upon the city's gates and the Temple that rose in sacred splendor beyond.

Equally amazing was the countless number of people who, instead of filling the road in mass movement to the Temple, formed unbroken lines that extended along both sides all the way to the city gates. There were many who ran ahead of Jesus, spreading their cloaks and other garments before him like miniature rainbows. There were others who cut and even pulled palm branches from the trees growing in the nearby fields. Some simply waved these branches in honor of his passing, and others, as those with the garments had done, laid the branches in his path so that the entire roadway before him was completely covered with palm branches and brightly colored clothing.

About then Ethan realized that not only was he not singing but almost all the other singing had ceased. In its place, the impassioned voices of the people beside the road rose and spread to the hills above with words and phrases that had been known and used since ancient times to praise and honor kings:

> Hosanna to the son of David.
> Hosanna in the highest.
> Blessed is he that cometh in the name of the Lord.

Shouted with equal conviction and fervor were direct acclamations of royal lineage:

> Blessed be the kingdom of our father, David,
> That cometh in the name of the Lord:

These declarations were reinforced with other outcries that clearly recognized and pronounced Jesus as their messianic king:

> Hosanna! Blessed is the King of Israel,
> That cometh in the name of the Lord.

> Peace in heaven, and glory in the highest.
> Blessed be the King that cometh in the name of the
> Lord;

These tumultuous praises, repeated over and over, rose with ever increasing ardor until Jesus' little procession entered triumphantly into Jerusalem.

28

Thoroughly fascinated, Ethan watched the entire proceeding. Although he continued in his descent with the others, he did so with total detachment. He was so overwhelmed by having just witnessed the fulfillment of a well-known prophecy, he was not even aware he was not alone in this remarkable drama. Yet, clearly, they all had seen an undeniable manifestation of what Zechariah the prophet foretold over 400 years before:

> Rejoice greatly O daughter of Zion; shout, O daughter of Jerusalem:

behold, thy King cometh unto thee: he is just and
having salvation; lowly and riding upon an ass, and upon
a colt the foal of an ass.

Eagerly, Ethan came to the end of his descent. Breaking free of the
others he almost ran to the nearest entrance to the Holy City. He felt
so sure that inside Jesus would declare his messiah ship and in some
miraculous way establish himself as king. Ethan's heart was pounding
almost to the breaking point as he rushed through the street leading to the
Temple and then into the outer courtyard of the Temple itself.

When he saw no sign of Jesus he felt a sense of alarm. His eyes darted
anxiously about. All he could see were the swarming masses of people
who did not appear to have been recently affected by any wondrous or
extraordinary event.

Emotionally, almost unable to speak, he approached a man closest to
him and asked, "Sir, do you know Jesus who came here a short while ago?
He was riding a young donkey."

To Ethan's utter amazement the man replied, very loudly and angrily.

"You better believe I know Jesus!" he exclaimed. "He was the one who
said he would save us. The Messiah! Ah, what a Messiah! He comes riding
in here on that donkey like he was fulfilling prophecy and what happens?
I'll tell you what happens. He gets mad with the people who are simply
tending to their business and proceeds to berate and deride them in the
worst kind of way. He tells them they have made his Father's house a den
of thieves. What blasphemy! He goes even further than that. He makes a
whip out of some cords, overturns their work tables and physically drives
them out of the Temple. He was like Samson, stronger than anyone I've
ever seen. No one could stop him. Those big fat money changers were
certainly no match for him. I guess being a carpenter, doing all that heavy
lifting and hard work made him that way. But by the time the Temple
guards got here he was gone. Just disappeared. Oh, yeah, I know your
Jesus. At least enough to know that he has deceived us and shattered all our
hopes and dreams of ever being free of Rome. What a fraud. They should
lock him up and throw the key away. If you're a friend of his, you better
be careful. They might just lock you up."

Others standing nearby gathered closer and they too angrily raised their voices against Jesus. Ethan could not believe what he was hearing. Just minutes before many of these same people had been laying their garments and palm branches down to cover Jesus' path into Jerusalem and sincerely shouting praises of him and acclaiming his majesty. Now, couched in threats to do him harm, he heard nothing but ridicule and scorn of Jesus. About then it became evident that if these angry people were unable to vent their feelings upon Jesus, then as his friend their animosity would fall upon him instead.

A realization of this possibility could easily have been more than sufficient to frighten Ethan, but he felt so discouraged, so downhearted he was oblivious to any danger. Perhaps those threatening him saw this as courage, even indifference to them or something else they respected. Whatever the reason, no effort was made to hinder him as he withdrew into the street, where he slipped inconspicuously into the bustling throng.

For a long time Ethan wandered aimlessly about the streets, jostled to and fro by the crowds, totally unaware of what was going on about him. One question plagued him relentlessly. If Jesus' entry into Jerusalem was not in fulfillment of prophecy, what was its purpose? As hard as he tried, he had no answer. Finally, he realized that remaining in Jerusalem would accomplish nothing. All he knew to do was return to camp.

29

It was still early in the evening when he arrived and was greeted by one of his friends who had been left to safeguard their belongings. The next day would be Ethan's turn to stand guard.

His friend sensed immediately that Ethan did not wish to talk and, suppressing his own desire to converse, he excused himself, saying he would go in search of firewood. Ethan simply replied that he would see him later and immediately sat upon one of the many large rocks that lay scattered about the campgrounds. In a barely audible voice filled with heartfelt fervor, he began to pray. After a time he got up and just wandered around, all the while continuing to pray. His prayer's one prevailing theme was for God to grant him understanding of all that was happening.

Ethan eventually resumed his seat upon the rock and was there when the others returned about an hour before sundown. They had heard about Jesus at the Temple that morning and told Ethan that because of it Jesus had apparently lost much of his following. So many were disappointed by what he had done. To them there was no apparent purpose for it. Everyone knew about the overcharging for the animals and the exorbitant exchange rates on the money, but that was the way it had always been. The former high priest, Annas, was probably the most corrupt of all. As testimony to that, the Temple market was often referred to as Annas' Bazaar. Even though officially Annas was no longer the high priest, the Romans having replaced him with his son-in-law, Caiaphas, he still exerted great control over Temple affairs and though leaving office he retained his title. He claimed the title was his, not Rome's. He was the one who decided what he would be called; there would just be two high priests. That presented no problem. Annas and his son-in-law worked well together. The fact that Jewish law provided for only one high priest was like other Jewish laws: when necessary they could be changed or ignored. Of course, such authority was not vested in everyone. Certainly not in someone like Jesus.

30

The evening meal was prepared and eaten, but with little being said. Everyone seemed absorbed in his own thoughts. Without the normal laughter and lighthearted conversation among the adults, the children, as though in deference to the sudden change in their parents' behavior, tempered their own cheerful nature and inherent playfulness accordingly.

Even the hills, which the night before had reverberated with such joyful songs and praises, now sounded pitifully subdued, evoking no joy, inspiration or comfort. In like manner, though there were the regular evening vespers, there appeared no real motivation to worship. Without any discernable reason, a saddened mood lay upon them all. In truth, the atmosphere, more funereal than celebratory, fit well with Ethan's own feelings.

Again Ethan lay in fitful sleep through the night and rose the next morning to virtual silence. There were pleasantries exchanged, but there was none of the gaiety and exuberance of the previous morning. Everyone was courteous but little else. The change was even apparent among the other Pilgrims as they wound their way down the hillsides to the road and on to the Temple. Regrettably, as it had been the previous night, the singing simply did not possess the psalmist's spirit of praise that in the past had urged believers to:

> Make a joyful noise unto the Lord, . . .
> Come before his presence with singing.
>
> Enter into his gates with thanksgiving,
> And into his courts with praise.

As the guard for the day Ethan remained in camp and felt relieved to see the others leave. For some reason he preferred being alone. His unanswered questions only compounded his feelings of helplessness and confusion. Even in his melancholy he wanted to think, and he felt a desperate need to pray.

As the day wore on, Ethan was deeply disappointed in finding little solace in either his thoughts or prayers, and that evening he actually welcomed the return of his friends. They were earlier than usual and attributed this to their concern about the growing unrest in the city. Again they were filled with rumors about Jesus. Not only did no one seem to know where he was, his apostles had apparently gone with him. The prevalent belief was they had all fled Jerusalem in fear of Annas and the Pharisees. Ethan hoped this was true.

During the evening meal a heated discussion arose about breaking camp and going home. The discussion continued for some time even after they had finished eating, but it was finally decided they would stay at least another day hoping that by then everything would return to normal.

The vesper service did even less to lift their spirits than it did the night before, and they all made their beds and retired to them as soon as they could. Several of them, like Ethan, would spend a restless and mostly sleepless night.

When he arose in the chill of a gray and gloomy dawn, Jesus was still uppermost on his mind. As he moved about tending to his personal needs he prayed for Jesus' and his apostles' safety.

During the night he had decided there was no longer any need to ask for answers to his questions. Why should he be so consumed with pleasing himself? Seeking self-satisfaction was not serving God. Certainly God knew what was on his mind and heart. Perhaps, he thought, this realization *was* God's answer. As he had done with the coins all those years, he would just have to wait.

Even though Ethan was somewhat reconciled to a state of "not knowing," he had no desire to return to Jerusalem, so he volunteered to stay and watch the camp again. As expected, no one objected. In fact, the only response was a simple "thank you" from the one whose place he'd take.

Ethan spent the day trying not to think of Jesus and everything that had happened. He found it hard to believe it had been just over a week; with so much going on it seemed much longer.

Clearing his mind of Jesus was not easy. Ethan knew that if Jesus remained in Jerusalem he was in serious danger, a possibility he could not ignore. From time to time he managed to think of his family, his son and his son's family. Then would come thoughts of his wife - - - lovely, beautiful Sarah, a wonderful wife and mother. Since her death, because of the heart-rending memories, he had tried to stifle such feelings. Now he let them surface. They had had such unbelievable, happy times together. No family had ever been more blessed, he thought. Appropriately, they had named their son Isaac. That they had no other children was just God's will. They never questioned it. They were so delighted He had blessed them with Isaac.

As the past drew him back to those happier times, his eyes misted over and a lump too big to swallow clogged his throat. With great effort he would think of something less personal. Then he would think again of Jesus and where he might be and the possible danger he faced if he were still in Jerusalem. After a while he found that the shifting back and forth between worry and resignation was itself disturbing, so once more when the others returned from Jerusalem, he was glad to see them.

Ethan's friends told him the situation in Jerusalem was really no better, but on the way to the camp, even with misgivings, they decided to remain another day. They did not believe Jesus was still in Jerusalem, and, if this were true, then everything should settle down.

The night passed pretty much as the previous three, and the next morning Ethan again agreed to stay behind. There were several tasks that had been neglected, and he spent the day tending to them. He had made friends with the man guarding the adjoining camp, and he agreed to keep an eye on Ethan's camp.

Ethan's first task was to replenish their water supply. There were two springs, one on the east and the other on the west side of the mount. Ethan understood that both were from the same source as the large stream that flowed through the Kidron Valley between the Temple Mount and the Mount of Olives. Although easier than going all the way into the Kidron Valley, it still required several trips to fill the large storage jar that had been previously placed in their area. This container held twenty baths and was almost empty. In appreciation of the guard in the adjacent camp, he filled the jar in his camp as well.

Next he attempted to find fire wood. By this time most all of the "blow down" was gone and after several hours he had found very little. At least by keeping busy, his mind was more at ease and, within minutes after he had finished bringing in the last of the wood he'd collected, his fellow campers arrived.

They reported that the whereabouts of Jesus and his apostles was still unknown, and contrary to what they had hoped, the public mood had not improved. Nevertheless, when they considered that the next day, Thursday, was the 14th of Nissan, the day of Unleavened Bread, when the Passover lamb had to be sacrificed, they realized they could not leave until Friday, the day after. This meant spending yet another night. All they could do was pray. Since it was the high point of Passover, by God's grace it would at least be peaceful.

In the meantime, they had another night that was very much like the others and even though the leaders tried, there was just too much missing and all of them were relieved when they could go to their respective places for rest.

The next morning Ethan announced that he would once more perform guard duty. He just wished there was more he could do. There was now plenty of water, and he was satisfied that going in search of firewood would be useless. Fortunately, they did not rely upon wood for their cooking but used charcoal which they had brought with them, and, if necessary, more could be purchased from the merchants in Jerusalem.

Without being gainfully occupied, Ethan simply walked about, spending much of the time becoming acquainted with the new guard in the other camp. He learned that this man was not familiar with Jesus, but had heard about him in Jerusalem, and, based on what he heard, believed Jesus was simply a troublemaker. Ethan was eager to explain how he personally knew Jesus and told him about all the marvelous things Jesus had done. Looking somewhat sheepish, the man asked Ethan to forgive his ignorance and thanked him for correcting his misconception. Then to Ethan's surprise, when their visit was over and he was walking away, the man, with genuine sincerity, said, "Sir, I really hope your Jesus is all right. I'll pray for him."

With just a slight hesitation, Ethan replied, "Sir, thank you for your concern, but Jesus is not mine. I believe he belongs only to God and was sent here by Him to do good for all of us. There's so much I do not know, but your prayers can only help and may God bless you for them."

31

It was late in the evening when the others arrived, extremely agitated. They told Ethan that Annas, the father-in-law of Caiaphas, the high priest, had ordered the Temple guards to arrest Jesus for blasphemy and for interfering with Temple business. It was reported, they said, that this was done by the instructions of Caiaphas himself, who, they also said, announced that for Jesus to die would be good for the people.

This news was so alarming to Ethan that at first, he could not speak. When he finally did, his voice was barely audible. With a low, hoarse cry, he groaned, "Why? Why? O God, You who are so compassionate and merciful. How can You let this happen?"

Too well he remembered the Pharisees' plot to kill Jesus and how this was what had brought him to Jerusalem. It was now apparent their plan was being carried out. Again there was nothing he could do. Somehow, from within his state of hopelessness, there emerged an intense desperation, and he knew he must try. Surely, he thought, now that action had been taken against him, Jesus' many disciples, and especially his apostles, would have a plan to help him, and he could join with them in carrying out their plan. Having decided there was hope after all, he was determined to do something.

When Ethan told his friends he must return to Jerusalem, they tried their best to discourage him. They warned that the hostility against Jesus could easily be turned upon him and all of Jesus' other friends.

Ethan briefly told them he was fully aware of the danger since he had already experienced it. In spite of that, he told them, he felt compelled to go. He would trust in God.

Seeing that he was determined, they ceased trying to change his mind and once more gathered around him, praying not only for God to protect him but also that Jesus would not be found. With many in tears and all in prayer, they saw him again descend the trail to Jerusalem.

32

Darkness had fallen by the time he reached the bottom of the trail, and though the moon had not yet risen, the stars were bright and with the lights of the city to guide him, he moved swiftly over the fairly level roadway to the nearest gate.

Once inside the walls he noticed nothing out of the ordinary. Just as they had been all week, the streets were filled with masses of people, mixing and mingling in constant motion. Without any discernable direction, they were much like sheep without a shepherd. As with sheep, he looked for some means to skirt the outer edges. In just minutes he saw an opening and went there as quickly as possible and proceeded to work his way into the city.

Having no idea where to find Peter or any of the other apostles, he moved at random about the streets inquiring as discreetly as possible about Jesus. Most of those he encountered simply turned away. He could only marvel at the difference now from when he first came to Jerusalem and merely mentioned Jesus' name. How popular Jesus was then! How eager people were to identify with him. Then, like a puff of smoke, his popularity had vanished.

It had grown late, past midnight, and suddenly there was boisterous commotion everywhere. Voices were loud and angry. A vast number of people were milling about in a jumbled, disorganized fashion, much like a mob. At some point this horde became one massive body and, like a swarm of bees, flowed down a street leading into the Essene Quarter.

Ethan, trying desperately to comprehend what was happening, found himself suddenly shoved tightly into the surging mass and unwittingly carried along by it to the palace of the high priest, where both Caiaphas and Annas resided.

In just minutes the huge crowd was halted by the massive gate of the palace, and Ethan was astounded to see Peter and another apostle, John, standing on the other side of the gate near the entrance of Annas' residence. Waving and shouting, Ethan pushed and shoved his way through the heavy press of bodies until he was finally seen by Peter and John who began waving and calling out to him.

Panting heavily, Ethan stopped at the gate. While he was wondering how he could get inside, John came forward and spoke to one of the soldiers. The soldier apparently gave an order to those at the gate and, just as the gate opened, he motioned for Ethan to enter.

Seeing the exhausted, worn appearances of John and Peter, made even worse by the dim, flickering firelight, Ethan was heartsick. When they told him Jesus had been arrested and was inside appearing before Annas, he broke down and wept.

What he had feared for so long had finally happened. He was crushed. Still there was nothing he could do. Feeling once more totally at a loss, he then remembered he had returned to Jerusalem in the hope that Jesus' disciples would have a plan. With this thought and having the attention of Peter and John, he was finally able to talk and find out what had happened.

John related how all of them had been together for the Passover Supper and then had gone to the Garden of Gethsemane, Jesus' favorite place, and it was there he was arrested. He described how Judas had pointed Jesus out to the Roman soldiers, presumably so there would be no mistake in identifying him. In telling this, John's tone was as bitter and angry as any Ethan had ever heard, and when he added that the Pharisees had paid Judas thirty pieces of silver for this treachery, the going price for a slave, he began sobbing.

Several moments passed before John was able to continue and, in a voice still quivering with emotion, he told about Peter's taking his sword and cutting off the right ear of one of the high priest's servants. Even though Judas' betrayal of Jesus was no worse than Ethan had feared, in hearing John's description of it, a raging fury came over him. In his mind's eye he could see Judas clearly at the gate of Simon the Leper with his thoroughly evil face twisted into that horrible, sinister leer. Had it been Judas, he knew he could have easily done to him what Peter did to the servant and even worse.

John continued, his speech faltered, "And . . . Ethan . . . you know . . . Jesus . . . just told Peter . . . 'put your sword away'. Then he touched . . . that bleeding place . . . where the ear had been . . . and . . . the ear just came back . . . like he'd never been hurt." Becoming too choked up to go on, John became quiet and just sadly shook his head. In witnessing John's heart-wrenching torment and visualizing Jesus in his infinite compassion healing the servant, Ethan's anger subsided.

When John could speak, he told Ethan how he and Peter had followed the band of soldiers with Jesus to the palace. Ethan then asked John about any plans they, and possibly the other apostles, had to help Jesus. John replied that they had no plan and he had no idea where the other apostles were. Ethan was stunned.

John explained that his father and the high priest were friends and that was how he and Peter were able to get through the gates. He could have gone into the house where Jesus was, but knew of nothing he could do if he did.

John said, "Annas is so corrupt . . . if only we had some money to bribe him. He doesn't care about the charge of blasphemy. That is just something to satisfy the Pharisees. What has made him mad is Jesus disrupting his business operation. He claims this is the second time and that seriously affects his purse. He's really mad and intends to end it once and for all. Unfortunately, we haven't anything to offer him."

Ethan said simply, "I do."

John, looking totally mystified, asked, "What in the world could you offer"?

Ethan replied, "At least three thousand shekels; probably more".

John was obviously overwhelmed. "Three thousand shekels!" he exclaimed. "A king's ransom!"

"Precisely," Ethan responded.

"And where," asked John, "are these shekels?"

"In a special pocket in my inner coat," Ethan answered, "I have three very large solid gold coins. Each one I have determined to be worth a thousand shekels or more."

John and Peter were elated, and after some discussion it was agreed that John would go into Annas' house and do what he could to arrange for the ransom of Jesus. They further agreed that under no circumstance would the source of the bribe be divulged. They also decided that the first offer would not exceed fifteen hundred shekels.

At the doorway was a woman whose job was to approve everyone who came into the house. She knew John so he was readily admitted, but when Peter attempted to follow, she refused to let him enter. John turned and spoke with her and at his insistence she told Peter he could go in. Then she asked him, "Aren't you also a friend of this Jesus?"

Ethan, standing close enough to hear, was astounded when Peter said, "No, I am not a friend of his." Because of his friendship with Peter, Ethan decided Peter had only said what he did in order to gain admittance. He did not approve, but he refused to believe that Peter was being disloyal to Jesus.

Ethan could see through the open passageway and saw Peter hovering over one of several large charcoal burners that warmed and brightened the inner courtyard. He could tell someone was talking to Peter, and he observed Peter's annoyed expression when he responded. A few minutes later another man obviously said something to Peter, and Peter's reaction was swift and angry. Ethan could see his face turn livid with rage and, though he could not understand the words, he could tell Peter was shouting. When he raised his hand and shook a finger in the man's face, the man jumped back and practically ran away. Immediately, a cock crowed.

As soon as this happened, the anger drained from Peter's face and he bolted panic stricken from the courtyard. Running as fast as he could past Ethan, tears streaming from his eyes, he screamed, "Merciful God, what have I done!"

Ethan had no time to reflect on what had happened. In just minutes John returned and Ethan could tell from his expression the news was not good. John told him their offer was taken to Annas but he rejected it. Annas had in effect scoffed at the offer, but did indicate he might consider a greater sum. John was apparently too upset to notice Peter's absence and, at that moment, Ethan saw no need to mention it.

Although they realized they would be bidding against themselves, they decided to offer the full amount, three thousand shekels, and John went back. As the time passed Ethan grew hopeful, but after about an hour his hopes were totally dashed. John appeared and sadly reported that Annas had rejected the second offer as well, saying it would have to be at least twice that amount.

Ethan felt utterly defeated. That was all he had. They could offer no more. They had been so in hopes the three coins would be sufficient. How anyone would refuse so much they could not understand. A hundred slaves could be bought for what they had offered and all they wanted was to buy just one man's freedom. No one would believe that Annas, for whatever perverted reason, would value that freedom so highly. Now there really was nothing else they could do, except make miserable, futile attempts to console each other.

33

Ethan did manage to tell John about Peter's running away and John was as puzzled as Ethan. However, their thoughts did not dwell upon Peter. Their real concern was Jesus and, befuddled as they were, he was uppermost in their minds. Being too distraught to think of anything constructive to do they just stood forlornly in front of Annas' house, watching it and waiting.

There was not long to wait. The huge, ornately carved double doors at the entrance suddenly swung open and a group of priests and members of the Sanhendrin led by Annas moved rapidly across the threshold into the courtyard. There followed a larger group composed mostly of Pharisees. They were all strangely quiet. Behind the Pharisees came a number of Roman soldiers forming a tight cordon around Jesus whose arms were bound tightly to his sides with a heavy rope. The ends of the rope were held by soldiers who took obvious pleasure jerking it first one way and then the other so that Jesus came stumbling awkwardly through the door way within plain view of Ethan and John.

Seeing Jesus humiliated by these Roman heathens in such a shameful, senseless manner only caused them to weep that much more. They felt their agony had reached its limit until they noticed Jesus' face and head, bruised, swollen and bleeding. His eyes were almost swollen shut and blood flowed from open cuts, matting his beard and hair with dark red streaks. His only clothing was a blood-spattered garment that had once been white. The sight was so shocking that not only Ethan and John, but many others cried out in utter disbelief at the horror they were witnessing.

John was so overcome he leaped toward the band of soldiers, wailing pitifully, "My Lord! My Lord! What have they done to you?" Immediately, one of the soldiers stepped toward him brandishing his sword. Fortunately,

Ethan reached him in time to pull him back. At that, the soldier returned to his position shouting a sharp warning for them to stay away.

In spite of the warning, Ethan and John followed the soldiers as they marched the short distance across the compound to the house of Caiaphas, where Annas and his group, the Pharisees and the soldiers with Jesus had gone. They saw all three groups enter the house and as they had done at Annas' house, they stood outside, sobbing in their misery and waited.

They watched a number of other men, including priests and members of the Sanhedrin, arrive and go inside. It appeared that the full body of the Sanhedrin was being assembled. To Ethan and John this meant Jesus was to be tried before the Sanhedrin. It tore at their hearts to think that these men who professed to be so good and obedient to God's law would punish someone who was truly good and had obeyed God's law perfectly.

Over the next two hours, the rose-tinted dawn spread slowly down the Mount of Olives into the sleepless city. In a matter of minutes, the trial would begin. Under Jewish law trials could only be held during daylight hours.

Now that a trial was imminent, John and Ethan sank into even deeper despair. Yet they stood steadfast, staring in frightful anticipation at the closed doors.

34

It was near mid-morning when the great doors to Caiaphas' house opened and those inside poured into the courtyard where the dazzling sunlight caused them to shade their eyes from the sudden brightness. They were no longer in separate groups, except for the soldiers who remained at the rear in a tight formation around Jesus. Most of those leaving the house followed in no particular order behind Caiaphas with several of the priests, but a number of others separated from the ones following Caiaphas and joined those who were waiting outside. They explained what had occurred inside and their account was terrifying. Contrary to what happened at Annas' house, the voices of those coming from the residence of Caiaphas had been loud and angry. Quite a few spoke out vigorously in favor of Jesus, but the majority were clearly those voicing opposition.

With increasing rancor Ethan noted that the trial was conducted just as the Pharisees said it would be. Hired witnesses testified falsely against Jesus, accusing him of blasphemy and of an additional charge of treason.

Both charges, especially that of treason, explained what was happening now. Caiaphas and the ones behind him were headed toward the Antonio Fortress, a palace where Pontius Pilate, Roman Governor of Judea, resided. The charges against Jesus were capital offenses, and even though the Sanhedrin could decide that a sentence of death was justified, only Roman authority could authorize the actual execution.

Jesus was still tightly bound and as he struggled to walk the soldiers resumed their merciless sport of pulling him off balance until he was falling and then snatching him upright again as viciously as they could. Not only did the soldiers take great delight in abusing him physically, they kept up a constant barrage of curses and ridicule, clearly expressing their intense hatred. Produced by training from an early age, this hatred was their strongest motivation; it became the terrible, irresistible force that made possible the success of Roman legions against Rome's enemies.

Yet, contrary to the way it appeared, the soldiers' hatred was not of Jesus. For him they had no feeling at all. Their hatred was its own self-fulfilling object. It sought only to be released. Merely suggesting that Jesus was an enemy turned the soldiers' hatred instinctively upon him. Even if Ethan and John had been able to understand this, it would have brought them no comfort, and their desolation and despair would have been no less. The vile and vicious mistreatment of Jesus would be the same.

What was now horribly apparent was that Jesus was in a far worse condition. As was obvious, he had been severely beaten again in the home of Caiaphas. The grim, heinous evidence was a face so swollen it had grown grotesque, its features distorted beyond recognition. Very little was left of the tattered garment about his body, leaving only strips of blood-soaked rags. Ethan and John could only look once upon this horror and turn away, striking their chests and crying loudly to God for mercy.

35

The fortress where Pilate resided was located across the city, just beyond the north wall of the Temple and some distance from the palace of Caiaphas. Already a large crowd was gathering and its numbers were steadily increasing. With Caiaphas at its head, the assembly of priests, Pharisees and members of the Sanhedrin, followed by the detachment of soldiers and Jesus, began to move in the direction of Pilate's residence. The crowd moved with them, creating for Caiaphas an intolerable situation. The roadway became blocked with the growing mass of people swarming wildly and loudly through the streets in front of Caiaphas and his group of followers. Acting quickly, Caiaphas ordered soldiers to come forward and clear a path through the unruly rabble. The soldiers dispatched for this task responded in true Roman fashion, ruthlessly and with exacting efficiency. Their brutal onslaught brought a swift dispersal of those causing the obstruction, and Caiaphas and his following proceeded unimpeded to the Fortress.

So they could be as close to Jesus as possible, Ethan and John remained in the rear, behind the soldiers. This way they avoided the turmoil of the multitude in front.

When they arrived at the Fortress, Caiaphas and those with him were allowed inside the outer wall, but they halted before the enormous timbered doors of the palace entrance that was securely guarded by soldiers on each side. Ethan and John, having followed so closely after the detachment of soldiers, were not stopped until the iron gate of the outer wall closed to block their entry. Even though they were pressed tightly into the throng that gathered around them they could easily observe what was happening to Jesus.

Because it was Passover, neither Caiaphas nor any of the others attempted to go inside. For a Jew to enter a Gentile dwelling rendered him ceremonially unclean, an act of defilement that required a seven-day cleansing process. Consequently, the commander of the soldiers with instructions from Caiaphas, consulted with a soldier at the entrance, and an order was given to admit him instead. In a few minutes he returned. After speaking to Caiaphas he then took Jesus, guarded by four other soldiers, and went again into the palace.

It was inconceivable to Ethan that Caiaphas and the chief priests would be more concerned about their ceremonial cleanness than their cold blooded, premeditated murder of an innocent man.

By this time a great multitude had assembled outside the fortress walls and, as time passed the noise became louder and louder. Purposeless, without leadership or organization, what had been no more than a large gathering of noisy people was quickly becoming an unruly mob.

Then Pontius Pilate, with Jesus and the five soldiers, appeared on the balcony above the fortress entrance. If the Jews felt defiled coming into his residence, Pilate would by no means go out to them. The balcony was ideal. From there he could talk down to them, and they were forced to look up to him. Amazingly, as soon as they appeared the deafening roar of the crowd subsided.

His voice resonating with authority, Pilate spoke firmly and distinctly. This was clear evidence of his other role as a military commander, properly titled Roman Prefect.

Looking at Caiaphas, Pilate asked him, "What accusation bring ye against this man?"

Caiaphas answered, "If he were not a malefactor, we would not have delivered him up unto thee."

Pilate replied, "Take ye him, and judge him according to your law."

To this Caiaphas replied, "It is not lawful for us to put any man to death." Pilate turned abruptly and re-entered the palace with Jesus and the soldiers following him.

After a short wait, but long enough for the people to resume their loud, unintelligible grumbling, Pilate with the soldiers and Jesus returned. As before, at their appearance the crowd became quieter.

This time Pilate, speaking more to the entire crowd than to Caiaphas and the chief priests, said, "I find in him no fault at all."

When Ethan and John heard this they turned to each other and laughed. Was it possible that this Roman ruler, who was best known for his cruelty and injustice, would release Jesus? For the first time during the entire ordeal there seemed to be some hope.

Their hope was short lived. A voice, which Ethan recognized as coming from one of the Pharisees, cried out, "He stirreth up the people, teaching throughout all Jewry, beginning from Galilee to this place."

When Pilate inquired and learned that Jesus was in fact from Galilee, he saw at once an opportunity to be relieved of an unpleasant task. Herod Antipas was tetrarch of Perea and Galilee. Technically, Jesus as a Galilean, would be subject to Herod's authority. Pilate knew that Herod was presently at his palace in Jerusalem, having come there for Passover. It was only a technicality, but one which Pilate thought could be quite useful and might even provide some amusement for him. He and Herod had never gotten along, and having Herod deal with the trouble Jesus had caused would please him immensely. Seeming reluctant and sounding as apologetic as he could, Pilate announced that he must deliver Jesus to Herod.

As Pilate and the soldiers guarding Jesus were leaving the balcony, there was a loud rumble of dissent from the people. Nevertheless, within a few minutes, Jesus, accompanied by his guards reappeared in the courtyard.

36

Herod's palace was located close to that of Caiaphas. This was some distance away and meant that the entire assembly of priests, Pharisees and the soldiers with Jesus had to go back the way they had come. Now, however, they were *followed* by the clamorous horde, which apparently had learned a lesson earlier from the soldiers.

Ethan and John managed to stay in front of the vast throng and were gratified to see that the soldiers were no longer yanking Jesus about. Evidently, even they could see he was barely able to walk and for him to keep falling and being pulled upright again was not only tiring for them, it had probably ceased to be fun.

As Herod was also a Jew, Caiaphas and his companions did not need to remain outside and were readily admitted into the palace. Later, Ethan and John learned that contrary to what Pilate thought, Herod was quite happy to see Jesus. He had wanted to see him for a long time and was especially hopeful that he could see Jesus perform some miracles. Even more ironic was that Pilate's seemingly inconsiderate gesture of sending Jesus to Herod laid the foundation for a lasting friendship between him and Herod.

Surprisingly, Caiaphas and his following did not stay long with Herod. After they exited the palace Ethan and John heard that Herod had attempted to interrogate Jesus, bombarding him with many questions, but Jesus refused to answer a single one. Also, Caiaphas and the chief priests made many accusations against Jesus to which he made no response. This so infuriated Herod, that he and his soldiers, after clothing Jesus in an old purple military cloak, made fun of him in the most reprehensible, loathsome manner, taking great delight in ridiculing and mocking him as a royal impostor. When they tired of their shameful and degrading sport, Herod ordered that Jesus be returned to Pilate.

Because of Pilate's previous indication that he believed Jesus to be innocent, Ethan and John were greatly pleased and relieved with this turn of events. They were also thankful that from all signs Herod had not physically abused him.

Something did bother them. In their return to the Fortress they saw a number of Pharisees and priests separate from those following Caiaphas and move to the rear of the procession. These interspersed into the enormous throng that tramped along noisily behind the soldiers.

Finally, when they had gotten back to the Fortress, Pilate, the soldiers and Jesus, still wearing the purple cloak, came out on the balcony. Pilate again addressed the boisterous assembly, saying to them:

> Ye have brought this man unto me, as one that perverteth the people; and behold, I, having examined *him* before you, have found no fault in this man touching those things whereof *ye* accuse him: No, nor yet Herod; for I sent you to him; and, lo, nothing worthy of death is done unto him. I will therefore chastise him, and release *him*.

This was necessary because it was customary during Passover that one prisoner be released.

To Pilate's proposal there was an enormous uproar from the crowd, which cried out, "Away with this *man*, and release unto us Barabbas." Every one knew that Barabbas was in prison for murder and for taking part in an insurrection in Jerusalem against Rome.

By this time Ethan and John knew that those Pharisees and priests, who were now circulating among the people, were agitating and inciting them to this outrageous demand. This was made easier by the large quantities of wine being consumed, for the more the people drank, the more belligerent and obnoxious they became.

Still there was hope. Pilate continued to try to change the people's minds, although the more earnestly he pleaded, the louder they protested, *"Crucify him! Crucify him!"*

Due to the increasing noise, Pilate's responses likewise grew louder, as though he were directing troops in battle. Challenging the barbarous protests from the crowd, he vehemently insisted on Jesus' innocence. Over and over he asked much the same question, and each time he answered it.

"Why, what evil hath he done?" He asked. "I have found *no cause* of death in him: I will therefore chastise him, and let him go."

Unquestionably, Pilate's intercession for Jesus was genuine. It was so sincere, so persuasive. Sadly, it was to no avail. By now the people in their hysteria had joined their voices into one blood chilling chant:

"*Crucify him, crucify him! Crucify him, crucify him! Crucify him, crucify him!*"

There were, however, some voices that could be heard above all the others. No words, only the mournful, heart rending screams and tearful wailing of women that pierced the angry, hate filled air. Still, it was not these, but the ones driven by their blood-thirsty lust, who would prevail.

37

Pilate finally ordered that Jesus be scourged. Scourging was a Roman method of whipping condemned criminals and slaves, usually preceding crucifixion. In itself an exceedingly cruel punishment, such an order seemed totally counter to Pilate's belief that Jesus was innocent of any wrongdoing. To anyone except Pilate it was. Desiring not only to free Jesus, but to appease the people as well, it was all he could do. If scourging alone would satisfy them, then he would at least have saved Jesus' life. That would be as close as he would ever come to doing what was right.

Scourging was done with a whip called a *flagrum* and consisted of a handle with two or three short thongs attached, usually of leather. Knotted at intervals along the thongs and at the ends were small pieces of metal, bone or other hard object. The *flagrum* was primarily designed to cause bruising. Scourging was administered by Roman soldiers known as *lictors*. A *lictor* received special training for this duty and knew how to wield the *flagrum* so as to open existing bruises and cause the blood to flow freely. More than one *lictor* was used to scourge each prisoner. They were trained so they could inflict blows simultaneously upon the shoulders, back, buttocks and legs.

According to Jewish law, a prisoner could receive no more than forty lashes. The Pharisees, always making sure the law was strictly kept, insisted that in the event an error occurred during the counting only thirty-nine lashes could be administered. Of course, if the error was greater than one, the law was still broken. Moreover, what apparently had not occurred to them, or else what they refused to consider, was that with a three thonged whip, each stroke of the whip inflicted not one, but three lashes. This of course meant that only thirteen strokes were needed to satisfy the thirty-nine-lash mandate. Failure of the Jews to apply this rationale resulted in the prisoner's receiving not thirty-nine lashes, but three times that number.

Yet, as cruel as scourging was by Jewish law, it was nothing compared to that of the Romans. Under Roman law there was no limit to the number of lashes. The only limitation was when the centurion in charge determined that further punishment would result in death. There were occasions, even when the victim fainted, if the *lictor* could feel his pulse and determine he was breathing the beating would continue. Because scourging was normally preparatory to crucifixion its object was to weaken the prisoner to the point of collapse and to bring him as near death as possible.

Extensive blood loss was most likely intended to shorten the victim's time on the cross. Crucifixion was the most brutal and cruelest form of public execution, designed not only to punish the violators of Roman law, but to instill such fear in those who witnessed it that they would blindly obey Roman authority and be far less likely to oppose its oppressive rule. Yet the success of this policy was far easier to prove in theory than in practice. At times roadways were lined on both sides with crosses on which mostly political prisoners were nailed. To carry out these pogroms, an enormous amount of wood was required. Due to a constant shortage of wood, this meant that crosses were reused. Reducing the time the victim remained on the cross allowed a faster turnover. The best conservation of wood could be credited to the many who did not survive the scourging administered by the Romans, who aptly named it the "half death."

Although incapable of proof, the torment and suffering inflicted by scourging was perhaps greater than that by crucifixion. The only absolute certainty was that both were immeasurably painful and horrible beyond description.

The scourging imposed by Pilate would be according to Roman law, not Jewish. In hearing this pronouncement, Ethan and John threw themselves prostrate upon the ground, striking it with their fists and groaning in unrestrained anguish.

Jesus was brought down to the courtyard where a full cohort of soldiers had been assembled. Forming itself around Jesus they marched with him to the rear of the Fortress to the praetorium, commonly known as the Judgment Hall. The praetorium contained a large area open to the public and it was here that the scourging would take place. Because the public was allowed to witness the punishment and many would observe this horrible spectacle, the heavy complement of soldiers, some 600, was needed to keep order.

The floor of the praetorium was paved with stone, hence another name, The Pavement, although the Jews called it Gabbatha. Rising out of the floor were several thick posts to which victims being scourged were tied. Jesus was taken to one of these posts. His wrists were bound together, raised above his head and secured to an iron ring in the post.

Ethan and John had struggled to their feet and in a dazed state of indescribable grief went with the cheering crowd to the praetorium. What they saw was more than they could bear. Jesus was securely affixed to the post, his face pressing against it. The few rags that remained about his body were stripped away so that only a bloody cloth covered his hips and loins. Two soldiers came towards him swishing their *flagrums* back and forth as though to acquire just the right feel of them. When they were close enough they stepped back, raising the whips over their heads ready to deliver the first blows. In seeing this Ethan and John fell again upon the ground wailing pitifully in agonized pleas for God to spare Jesus this evil, senseless suffering.

They did not look, but too vividly they heard the whistling and cracking sound of the whips as they tore through the skin into the sinews and muscles of Jesus' near naked body. They could only imagine the waves of excruciating pain that coursed through his body as blow after blow was delivered.

The crazed, angry mob which had demanded Jesus' crucifixion now watched with great delight this gruesome, savage display. They cheered and shouted encouragement to the *lictors,* taking great pleasure in seeing the rupture of bruises as the *flagrums* tore them open and blood oozed, spurted and then flowed down Jesus' body and legs to form an ever-expanding crimson pool about his feet. His entire backside quickly became a bloody mass of ripped and torn flesh. The metal and bone particles cut deeper and deeper into the muscle and bone until strips of flesh tore loose. Massive tremors radiated from exposed raw nerves to every part of his body carrying with them an incessant pain that was so intense, so severe it was inconceivable that anyone could endure it.

At last Jesus' legs gave way and only his wrists secured tightly to the post kept him from falling. Violent spasms racked his body, then suddenly they ceased. Perhaps believing he was dead, the *lictors* stopped the beating. Jesus was untied and collapsed upon the bloody pavement. Throughout the entire ordeal Jesus never uttered one sound, not even the slightest whimper or sigh.

There was now complete silence, and no longer hearing the terrible strokes of the whips, Ethan and John looked up to see the crumpled form of Jesus, that from shoulders to feet lacked resemblance to anything other than a large red lump of freshly hacked meat. Too horrified even to scream, they could only stare at the grisly sight, their minds recoiling, incapable of accepting what they were seeing, but knowing it was all too real.

Unbelievably, in a few minutes Jesus was able to recover some of his strength and looked up at his tormentors in the most compassionate, forgiving way imaginable. Unwilling to look at him they immediately turned their heads.

The poignant effect upon Ethan and John was overwhelming. Yet, in spite of their feeling and for a reason he could not explain, as Ethan looked upon the ravaged figure of Jesus lying there on the blood-drenched pavement he was reminded of a scripture passage written by the prophet Isaiah hundreds of years before. He had never associated the passage with any particular person, but he could see now it was as though Isaiah was witnessing this very scene when he wrote:

> Even as many were amazed at him—so marred was his look beyond that of man, and his appearance beyond that of mortals

38

Numbed into a state of absolute despair, Ethan and John watched the soldiers drag Jesus away into the inner chambers of the Hall. After some time they reappeared with him, and to everyone's astonishment, Jesus was standing upright, although in the most pathetic condition. A crown of gigantic thorns had been crudely plaited and pressed upon his head.

Fresh blood flowed freely from the wounds in his scalp down his face to add more blood to his already saturated beard and to trickle across the bare patches where his beard had been ripped away.

The soldiers had also replaced the purple cloak over his shoulders. As they stood around him, they struck him with reeds and spat upon him. Some knelt in mock fashion around him and cried out, "Hail, King of the Jews!" All the while they continued to smite him with the reeds and slap and hit his face with their hands and fists. During all of this vile mistreatment, Jesus stood like a statue, silent and still. Even with his face swollen and mutilated beyond recognition he appeared perfectly composed, making not the least effort to avoid any of their vicious abuse. This infuriated his tormentors all the more.

What he was now seeing caused Ethan to recall another passage from Isaiah:

> I gave my back to the smiters, and my cheeks to them who plucked off the hair; I hid not my face from shame and spitting.

After several minutes Pilate came out and signaled the soldiers to withdraw. Stepping forward he stood beside Jesus. With palm up he extended his hand towards Jesus and boldly declared to the angry assembly, "Behold the Man!"

The immediate response was the deafening renewal of previous demands. "Crucify him! Crucify him!" they screamed.

To this, Pilate shouted back, "Take ye him, and crucify him; for I find no fault in him!"

For some reason Caiaphas was not present, but one high priest speaking as loudly as he could, replied, "We have a law, and by our law he ought to die, because he made himself the Son of God."

Pilate was visibly shaken by this charge. So much so that after giving an order to the soldiers he withdrew into the Judgment Hall to be followed promptly by the soldiers pulling Jesus along with them.

39

When Pilate returned, he was alone. He made repeated attempts to persuade the people to be satisfied with the punishment Jesus had already received, reminding them that as they could all see, Jesus had already been severely beaten before he was scourged.

Regrettably, to Pilate's growing frustration, each attempt was scornfully rejected with the all-too-familiar cry:

Crucify him! Crucify him!"

Another chief priest standing not far from Pilate cried out, "If thou let this man go, thou art not Caesar's friend; whosoever maketh himself a king speaketh against Caesar."

For good reason this seemed to upset Pilate more than anything else. Even Rome lacked the resources to maintain large military garrisons in its many outlying provinces and was only able to maintain order in these by instantly crushing the first sign of rebellion with brutal retaliation. The governors of the provinces, such as Pilate, had one primary responsibility--keeping the peace, a peace universally known as *Pax Romana,* the Roman peace. It was not a genuine peace, as it was established and maintained by unmerciful force, which by totally suppressing offenders would terrify everyone else into submission. Unfortunately for Pilate, it had not been as effective in Judea as it had in the other regions. Already there had been several instances of violent civil disobedience, such as that joined in by Barabbas.

During Passover, Jerusalem was overflowing with Jews from all parts of the Empire, making it extremely vulnerable to an uprising. A large-scale riot was something Pilate could not afford and would not risk. Tiberius Caesar would not tolerate one and if one did occur, it would most assuredly cost Pilate his job and very likely his life.

In any event, Pontius Pilate knew that Jesus was not a threat to Rome or to Caesar and most certainly not to the Jews. He also knew what would be the right thing to do. Because he was a coward, he would not do it.

As he had done many times before, Pilate walked with deliberate solemnity to the large marble Judgment Seat erected upon a raised stone platform, known as the *bema,* located in one corner of the Pavement. Judgment Seats were used by Roman magistrates and other officials who possessed authority to pronounce judgments in all matters brought before them. Rendering a judgment from the Judgment Seat was deemed to give the decision both validity and finality.

Pilate's mounting the steps of the *bema* to the Judgment Seat meant he was going to render his judgment. Once he was seated, he ordered Jesus to be brought out.

40

Led to the foot of the *bema* by his guards, Jesus was left standing there to face all those who were clamoring for his death. Even in his wretched state, there was an aura about him that defied such pathos. The crown though made of thorns, and the cloak, though old and tattered, were made to appear by his regal bearing emblems of majestic grace. Motionless he stood, perfectly straight, head high, dignified in every respect. There was not the least indication of anger, fear or uncertainty. Throughout all the rigors of his torture he had endured the terrible pain without complaint. Not a murmur had escaped his lips. He demonstrated conclusively to everyone, that there was nothing man could do to him that he feared, and, moreover, that he was in total control of his mind and body. He appeared as though everything that had happened had been just the way he had planned it and wanted it to be.

It would have been impossible for Pilate not to have recognized that he was not dealing with an ordinary man. Without question the suggestion that Jesus might be the Son of God was something he had to consider. Unfortunately, this consideration became much less important when it was further suggested he might displease Caesar.

Nevertheless, even though he had taken the Judgment Seat, Pilate was still perplexed and unsure of what to do. He did try once more to convince the huge mass of people, who were now on the brink of riot, that Jesus should be set free, saying to them with as much conviction as he could muster,

BEHOLD! YOUR KING!

Obviously unwise, this approach served only to intensify the people's anger, which they loudly demonstrated at the top of their lungs,

AWAY WITH HIM! AWAY WITH HIM! CRUCIFY HIM!

Making one last attempt, equally unwise, Pilate asked, "Shall I crucify your King?" To this the chief priests shouted almost in unison, "We have no king but Caesar!"

Again the reference to Caesar hit a nerve. Pilate gave up. He issued an order, and in moments, a bowl of water was brought to him. While a servant held the bowl, Pilate dipped his hands into it and bathed them. When he raised his hands dripping with the clear, glistening liquid, he held them up as though he wanted everyone to see they were not stained with blood. Then in a rather subdued voice he declared, "I am innocent of the blood of this just man; see *ye* to it."

Immediately, a loud, jubilant cry went up, "His blood be on us, and on our children."

Pilate thereupon ordered that Jesus be taken to Golgotha where he was to be crucified. He next directed that Barabbas be released. At this announcement the people cheered ecstatically. Ethan and John, absolutely devastated, leaned upon each other sobbing and begging God to save Jesus from this horror.

Jesus was led back inside the Judgment Hall where he would be prepared for the march to Golgotha. Upon Jesus' leaving, Ethan and John began talking to each other, realizing that so far they had overindulged in their own self pity. It was John who suggested that Jesus would expect them to be strong and not be overcome by grief. Though it almost brought him again to tears, John avowed that Jesus had given them a perfect example of how they should act and that there must be something they could do.

At first they considered finding the other apostles or perhaps just some friends, but they decided that would serve no purpose. Even if they found them, they would be of no value to Jesus. If they could have been any help, they would have already done something.

Evidently the thought of such futility caused John to think of their attempt to buy Jesus' freedom from Annas. Reaching inside his cloak he produced the three gold coins. Holding them out to Ethan he said, "You know, I had completely forgotten about these." Ethan shook his head and replied, "No, you keep them, John. Perhaps you will find a good use for them. Jesus said that I would, but I'm afraid I won't." John could tell that it would serve no purpose to argue with him and without saying anything else he put the coins back in his cloak.

They were quiet for several minutes. Finally, John exclaimed, "I know what I must do!"

"What is that?" Ethan asked.

"It's Jesus' mother," John replied. I have to see about Mary. How terrible this has to be for her. I must find her and try to help."

Ethan said, "You are right. I'll go with you."

"No," said John, "I think it will be better if I go alone. If Jesus can see you along the way, perhaps it will give him some comfort. Perhaps you can even say something to him."

Ethan had no idea what he would be able to say and thought John would be a more welcome sight to Jesus, but before he could say anything, John was gone.

41

Golgotha, the usual place for crucifixions, was a rocky knob very much resembling a human skull; it was aptly named Golgotha, which means, "the place of a skull." Just a short distance northwest of the praetorium, it overlooked both the Fortress and the Temple.

Although Ethan had never before followed the entire process of someone's being crucified, several times he had seen the wretched creatures struggling along to their executions, always bearing their own crosses. For them he knew it was not just a short distance to Golgotha. It was instead a grueling, shameful, hopeless climb that would only end in unimaginable pain and death. The sight always aroused in him a bitter anger towards Rome and profound sorrow for those miserable souls so fiendishly wasted, though what he felt in the past was nothing compared to what he felt now.

He recalled what John had said and prayed briefly for God to strengthen him and give him the courage to do whatever could be done to help, realizing he was still at a loss as to what that might be. Sadly shaking his head, he went with the many others to where the soldiers with Jesus would come out on the road to Golgotha.

To Ethan's surprise, when the large doors of the praetorium opened, it was not Jesus who emerged, but another prisoner with the customary four guards that made up the standard crucifixion detail. Behind this group came yet another, and Jesus was not in it either.

But he was in the next one. Like the first two, a cross was placed over his shoulder so that the piece where his hands would be nailed extended in front of his body almost to the ground and upwards some three feet above his head. The longer section trailed behind with its end dragging through the dirt.

Until Jesus' appearance, the spectators on both sides of the road were saying very little. Then, as soon as they saw Jesus, the air became filled with not only the angry, threatening voices that had demanded his crucifixion, but equally as loud were the piteous shrieks and wailing of women and even men whose hearts were about to burst. It was more than Ethan could take. He too broke down, joining the others in their pathetic cries of hopeless devastation. All thoughts of being strong and courageous vanished.

Ethan could see that Jesus had been re-clothed in his own cloak with the beautiful white linen vesture covering his body from his neck to his feet. That his garments had been carefully preserved was undoubtedly due to Roman law which awarded the victim's clothing to the soldiers who carried out the crucifixion. Though unintended and of no consequence to the soldiers, the grieving spectators were at least spared for a time the sight of Jesus' hideously mutilated body.

When Jesus faltered or failed to move as fast as they desired, the soldiers struck him viciously with the heavy sticks they carried, all the while cursing and vilifying him. True to their character they did not use whips--clearly not wanting to tear "their" clothing.

After all the beating and physical punishment Jesus had suffered, his incredible strength and stamina finally played out. Beneath the great weight of the cross he collapsed. Immediately the soldiers fell upon him, wielding their clubs with an insatiable fury.

Suddenly there appeared a centurion on horseback. Angrily he ordered the beating to cease. His face livid with rage, he shouted at the guards, "Rome does not crucify dead men!" He then directed one of the soldiers to impress a man from the spectators to help carry Jesus' cross.

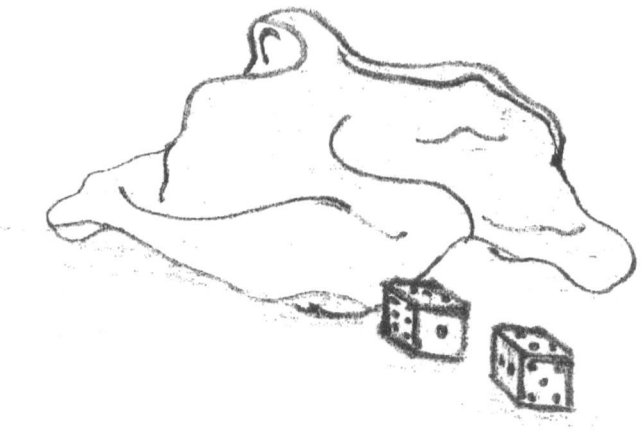

Perhaps not hearing the centurion's command, the man selected began to resist. His wife standing next to him cried out in a frightened voice, "Simon, what are they doing?" Bursting into tears she screamed at the soldier, "Leave him alone! Leave him alone!"

In spite of his resistance, the man was quickly subdued. Then as the soldier pulled him toward Jesus, he realized what he had been chosen to do. With a willing cry he broke free of the soldier's grasp and, running to Jesus, lifted the cross from his shoulder. Even though Jesus was able to stand, he still held to the cross and refused to move aside for the man called Simon to take his place. With Jesus' refusal to relinquish the heavier part to him, Simon, who was so willing to help, could only move behind Jesus where his part of the burden would be lighter. From there he followed Jesus to Golgotha.

42

Ethan stood some distance away on top of the barren knoll but still was able to observe the crosses being erected. He could not see them, but knew the crosses would be inserted in holes which had been used many times before. Each cross was laid so its lower end rested on the edge of a hole. The cross with the body would require all twelve guards to raise it.

Once the crosses were laid in place, those to be crucified were stripped of all clothing, except for some coarse rags that barely covered their loins. Each victim was placed on his back upon the long beam, with his arms stretched out along the shorter one.

While held by his executioners, seven-inch spikes were driven with heavy iron mallets through Jesus' wrists and feet into the rough, hard wood. As with all the previous torture and pain he had suffered, Jesus withstood this barbaric atrocity with the same calm restraint. Groaning and weeping profusely, Ethan fell face down upon the ground to blot from sight just more horrifying evidence of man's depravity.

The two criminals being crucified with Jesus were not nailed to their crosses. Instead, they were simply tied to them by their wrists and ankles. Although this was much less painful than being nailed, death usually took much longer. It may have been considered either a less severe punishment or more severe, depending on the opinion of the sentencing official and the reason for his judgment. It is conceivable that these two crosses had been used so much the nails would no longer hold.

Regardless of the method, death by crucifixion was normally caused by the victim's being slowly strangled. The weight of the body created a tremendous strain upon the wrists, arms and shoulders, usually resulting in dislocation of the shoulder and elbow joints. The downward pull of the body made it very difficult to exhale and impossible to take a full breath.

To breathe at all, the victim had to push himself upward from his feet to relieve the pressure on his throat. Over a period of time, the pain and exhaustion became too much and he either gave up or fainted. Then it was only a short while before he suffocated.

When the three bodies were secured to the crosses a long rope was looped around the one to which Jesus was nailed. Four soldiers standing in front grasped the rope and pulled, while at the rear the other eight lifted the cross until it slipped into the hole in an upright position. The process was repeated twice again and, in minutes, with Jesus between the other two, all three crosses were raised to look out upon Jerusalem in stark reproof of Jewish and Roman justice.

43

Most all of those who so eagerly had sought Jesus' death, especially the priests and Pharisees, swarmed angrily about his cross. Even though Ethan could not hear what they were saying, he could tell from the movement of their hands and the tone of their voices that they continued to mock and revile him.

Apparently, when Jesus did not respond to their taunts and ridicule, they realized there was no other way they could hurt him so they began to slip away, one, two and three at a time until only a few remained. Whether they felt cheated, ashamed, satisfied, pleased or indifferent, to Ethan their guilt was the same. His own feeling was an intense loathing for them all.

Fervently he beseeched God to put upon them all the pain and suffering their evil deserved, which he reverently insisted should be far worse than what Jesus had undergone. What would be worse he could not imagine, but he knew that whatever torment or torture man could devise would not suffice for what they had done.

When many of Jesus' tormentors had withdrawn, a number of Jesus' followers, mostly women, came closer, some kneeling and others falling prostrate in heartrending anguish upon the ground before him. In witnessing their intense grief and heartache so visibly and vocally expressed, Ethan's outrage suddenly ceased. Just as quickly, with the passing of his rage went all hope as well, leaving the forlorn emptiness that comes only from the deepest sorrow and despair.

Somehow, in spite of his wretched state, Ethan recalled vividly a beautiful spring morning in Galilee about a year before when he sat with many, many others upon a mountain side, with the grass flowing thick and green down the gentle slope. They had all gathered there filled with eager anticipation to hear Jesus.

Jesus' message that day was the most marvelous Ethan had ever heard. It was more like a sermon. He remembered so well Jesus' describing how they should live in harmony with each other. He told them they should be humble and treat each other with justice and mercy. Also, they should strive for peace and live good, clean lives. In very positive terms he said they should treat others as they wanted others to treat them. There was so much that was so appealing you really wanted to live as he said you should, although Jesus warned them it would not be easy. In fact, he stressed that those who followed him and his teaching could expect to be severely persecuted for it. Even so, he assured them that by living their lives according to his commandments, they would receive blessings that would wipe away even the memory of persecution. Everything he said sounded so wonderful.

Ever since then Ethan had often wondered why the instructions of the scribes and Pharisees were never like those of Jesus. They always preached the same thing--strictly obey the law or suffer terrible consequences for disobedience. Even though a mandate of the great commandment was to love your neighbor as yourself, seldom was it mentioned in their teaching and even less often did they practice it.

Then it came to him why his thoughts had turned to that spring day in Galilee. It was now so obvious what Jesus had done. He was the living example of what he taught, especially during the last several hours. Courageously facing his tormentors and enduring the worst torment they could inflict, he demonstrated in the most painful extreme what he meant when he said:

> But I say unto you, that ye resist not evil; but whosoever shall smite thee on thy right cheek, turn to him the other also.

Regrettably, no comfort came with his understanding. Ethan remained disconsolate. Had it been possible, he would have been even more distraught. He knew he would never be able to forgive those who, without any justification, viciously murdered an innocent man whose sole purpose was to do good.

44

Ethan moved closer to the crosses. He could now read what was written on a sign above Jesus' head. Printed in large letters in Hebrew, Latin and Greek were the words, "JESUS OF NAZARETH THE KING OF THE JEWS". Under Roman law, public notice stating the offense and the name of the offender was required in all crucifixions.

Dumbfounded, Ethan shook his head bitterly in disbelief. Rather than stating an offense the notice was just another way for Rome to express its disdain for the Jews. This inevitably brought to mind something equally as bitter. After all the treachery, the travesty of a trial and the unbelievable torture, *Rome's final resolution for Jesus was for him to be convicted and crucified for no crime at all.* Ethan would one day realize that what Pontius Pilate had cravenly refused to acknowledge in Jesus' life, he had intuitively recognized and proclaimed in his death.

The shrill shrieks and screams of the women that earlier had been raised spontaneously in anger and fright at the seemingly endless scenes of horror and terror passing before them, had subsided. They now clutched each other in prayer and deep convulsive sobs of sorrow.

Ethan recognized Jesus' mother, Mary, standing just beneath Jesus with John's arms wrapped about her. Jesus appeared to be speaking to them, but Ethan could not understand what he said. With them, he also saw Mary's sister and Mary Magdalene from whom Jesus had cast out many demons, so that thereafter she became one of his most devoted followers.

Seeing them reminded Ethan of Mary and Martha and their brother, Lazarus, in Bethany. He wondered if word of this terrible tragedy had reached them, and, if it had, he knew how heartbroken they would be.

As he began to look for them in the crowd, he became aware that the light had been slowly fading. A dusky gloom was beginning to settle over the landscape. Distant terrain features were barely visible. Those that were closer had likewise grown dim.

Ethan had no idea what was happening. It was not a fog. There were not even any clouds. Being only an hour or so past mid-day, the Roman sixth hour, the sun was still almost directly overhead. It just simply did not appear as bright as it should be.

After a while the crosses were only three identical blurs rising above the people huddled about them. The people themselves had merged into a much larger blur without discernible shapes or features. Even if Mary, Martha and Lazarus were there, he would not be able to recognize them.

About the ninth hour Ethan moved even closer, instinctively straining to see what he had no desire to see, but compelled for some reason to try. The vast gray shadow now enveloped everything around him, seemingly emanating from the three near-lifeless forms hanging as grotesque silhouettes from their crosses. As painfully perplexed as he was, Ethan remembered the psalm of King David and what he said about "the valley of the shadow of death." He wondered if what was happening could be such a valley. Before he could really consider this thought or David's assurance that even if it was, there was nothing to fear, the brief spell of his reverie was abruptly broken. Out of the ominous gloom, above and beyond all the other sounds and voices, came a sorrowful, agonized cry:

"ELOI, ELOI, LAMA, SABACHTHANI"

Immediately, Ethan knew that not only was it Jesus who had spoken, but knew as well the foreboding meaning of that cry:

"My God, My God, Thou Hast Forsaken Me!"

The gravity of this lament was so grievous, so terribly distressing that Ethan trembled. His trembling only intensified when he heard Jesus cry out again:

"FATHER, INTO THY HANDS I COMMEND MY SPIRIT!"

At the instant these words were uttered, the ground shook and a sudden wind tore severely across the bare, unyielding rock. A sinister chill gripped him. The sky turned black and what was left of the sun seemed to be simply blown away. The darkness wrapped like a thick shroud about him. Except for the dark he could see nothing. As it was not yet night, there was not even light from the moon or stars.

Strangely, instead of fright, Ethan's immediate thought was that his blindness was like that of the Egyptians when the plague of darkness fell upon them. What he did not know was that this darkness was not a plague wrought by God. The simple and tragic truth was that, with the utterance of Jesus' last heartrending cry, the light of the world went out.

45

Supernatural though it was, evoking many loud frightened cries of alarm and distress from those assembled on that bleak hill, for Ethan it held no fear. Perhaps it was the assurance King David had promised. More likely it was just that after everything else that had happened mere darkness posed no threat or danger. In a sense it was the closest to any comfort he would feel, for at least it shielded him from the horrible sight of the crosses. He did not believe that either death or harm was imminent. His deepest feeling was one of profound sorrow and loss. His spirit was so low death might have come as a welcome relief.

Even so, as he had always done in times of grief and distress, he fell to his knees in prayer. At first no words came. Then he simply confessed his complete loss in all that was happening and humbly prayed for God's mercy and sustaining grace.

Soon after they began, the earth's tremors ceased. It was not long before the bright sunlight returned, and Ethan was able to see everything that was taking place. The Roman soldiers removed the crosses from the holes and laid them on the ground. They produced heavy iron mallets and proceeded to break the legs of the ones who had been crucified. However, when they came to Jesus, instead of breaking his legs a soldier simply pierced his side with a spear. Ethan knew no reason for this, but he recalled that the prophets Isaiah and Zechariah had spoken of the coming Messiah's body being pierced. Other than this he had no explanation for what was happening.

Once the soldiers had completed their gruesome work, those who remained began to slowly disperse, continuing to raise their grief-stricken voices in prayer and soulful lamentation. Even after the bodies were removed from the crosses and carried away, Ethan stood for some time, staring transfixed at the forsaken spot where so much horror and sorrow had so recently been joined. He finally decided that there was nothing else to do but return to his friends at their camp above Jerusalem.

Without even realizing how, he found his way back to the camp, and upon arriving he discovered no one else was there. Learning from the neighboring camp that his fellow campers and companions left the day before, he collapsed on the ground, tattered and torn in mind and spirit. Openly and unabashedly, he cried. In his mind all was lost. Sorely defeated and without even a fight, disappointed to the point of absolute despair, Ethan spent a sleepless and troubled night. The next morning, he packed his meager possessions and left for Galilee and home.

Traveling light and alone with a mercilessly heavy heart, he pushed himself to the point of total exhaustion, covering thirty or more miles a day. In just a little more than three days he was back in Galilee in his own home, weary and heart sick. He visited his son and his family and other friends, sharing very little with them about what had happened in Jerusalem. He did whatever he could to stay busy, cleaning, repairing, mending, anything to keep from thinking of Jesus, but he could not.

His thoughts turned constantly to Jesus. In brief unstructured sequence thoughts and memories flooded his mind:

The pronouncement of the angels on that cold winter night. Jesus as an infant; how perfect he was. Mary and Joseph. The Magi; their firm belief that Jesus was a saviour sent by God. The same hope and belief his father had. Jesus, a man as he knew him, kind, gentle, encouraging, compassionate, caring and above all, loving. How absolutely extraordinary he was. All he said and did, so eloquent, wise and comforting. So helpful to those in need, healing the sick and infirm. Openly speaking out against the oppressive tyranny of authority, its constant mistreatment of the poor, downtrodden and weak. So apparent that he was right and they were wrong. Fearless in his opposition to the authorities. How they loathed him for it and in the end they murdered him. At Simon the Leper's where Mary had paid Jesus such a beautiful selfless tribute; where Jesus had blessed him and so deeply touched him--- even his very soul. Jesus was so good in every way. How could anyone turn against someone so good? Yet, they did.

For the evil and hatred shown by Judas and the Pharisees, Ethan had no answer, and thinking about it was almost more than he could bear.

Later he would wonder why his anger did not totally consume him, and he decided he was just too miserable to feel anything else. His father had been filled with hope, and hope had been a certainty in his life as well. Now there was nothing.

46

About a week after Jesus had been crucified, Peter came to Ethan's home early one morning. Ethan's surprise at Peter's arrival was nothing compared to his astonishment at his appearance. Ethan's last recollection of Peter was his terror-stricken face as he fled across the courtyard at Annas' house. Now he was ecstatic, unbelievably exuberant. Before Ethan could even greet him Peter shouted, "Ethan! Good News! He lives! Jesus is alive!"

This was more than Ethan could grasp. He staggered against the doorpost, gripping it as tightly as he could. He struggled for breath but finally gasped, "Jesus alive? I don't believe you. You're mad. It's not possible!"

"I know," Peter replied. "Not for us, but praise God; for Him all things are possible."

With a touch of anger Ethan retorted, "I don't even know if you were there but I was." His voice broke. "I *saw* him die. Rome does nothing better than kill people. They not only crucified him, they drove a spear deep into his side. There is no way he could be alive."

"I know, I know," said Peter. "But all I say is true. Come with me and see for yourself."

Ethan did not and could not believe Peter at first. What Peter said was far more than he could even imagine. Yet he had seen Jesus perform many miracles, and he knew Jesus had brought Lazarus back to life. Perhaps, just possibly, Peter was telling the truth. As Peter said, with God all things were possible. Suddenly he felt a glimmer of hope.

In spite of his doubt, he went with Peter, feeling his heart quicken with anticipation as they walked along. Peter talked incessantly. He told Ethan the reason he had been so upset at Annas' house. Then, with great pleasure, he told how Jesus had forgiven him. Ethan said nothing, but the more Peter talked, the more hopeful he became.

They did not have far to walk and soon they were at the foot of a low-lying hill. As though it were only a few weeks past, Jesus sat upon a rock talking to a large number of people seated on the grass in front of him. The instant Ethan saw him his heart began racing, then almost stopped beating. His knees buckled. He nearly fell. Barely able to breathe and unable to move, torn between feelings of belief and disbelief, he stood in awe-stricken wonder at what he saw. There in the flesh was what he knew was impossible. Yet there he was.

Speaking very much in the same voice and manner as he always had, so calm and self-assured, in the kindest and most caring way, Jesus clearly expressed his love for all those gathered there. It sounded so familiar and, as Ethan recovered, he went closer. Listening intently, he could detect a different quality in Jesus' voice. There was more concern, a note of urgency. Nevertheless, Ethan knew it was Jesus. Of this he had no doubt.

He now knew how Mary and Martha felt when their brother emerged from his tomb alive. What joy, to know someone you believed dead is alive. How much greater is the joy, when it is someone you love. At that moment Ethan realized that that was his feeling for Jesus. How else could he have reacted as he did to all of Jesus' suffering and final death if he did not love him? Tears poured from his eyes, and he could no longer restrain himself. Without any thought of his intrusion, he rushed forward and fell prostrate at Jesus' feet. There with all the passion he possessed he exclaimed, "My Lord! My Lord! You are alive! O Thank You, Almighty God! Thank You most merciful and loving Father! Thank You! Thank You!" When he became too choked up to say any more, Jesus did as he had done at Simon's. He stood and reached down to Ethan with both hands. Just as it was then, Ethan rose to his knees and fervently grasped Jesus' hands. Once more he felt the rush of elation and the deep restful peace, which again left him with that wonderful feeling of contentment.

The rest of the day Ethan spent in a near euphoric state of reverence. As he pondered many of those same events that had disturbed him so much during his return from Jerusalem, he smiled. Were it not for the terror and horror he had witnessed and the thoughts of how much Jesus had suffered, he would almost be amused. Everything now made so much sense. Jesus knew exactly what He was doing.

Even the Magi knew that Jesus came not only to save the Jews, but all mankind. And it wasn't deliverance from Rome or any other human authority, either, but from Satan, who, with his pervasive infestation of sin was man's greatest enemy. Never had Jesus been under the power and control of the priests and Pharisees or Herod or Pilate. They were all under His control and being used by Him. Even Caiaphas' saying Jesus should die for the good of the people was God's decision, not Caiaphas'. It was God's will that prevailed, not theirs. They were merely petty, weak vassals of Satan.

Jesus was indeed the Messiah, the Christ, but even more than that. Martha was right. He was the Son of God. And what better way to attain God's saving grace could there be? Certainly, a father is most accessible through his son. It was something his own father had evidently known and had cherished until the day he died. This sudden thought actually startled him, striking him with the forceful impact that unexpected truth often has. Yet this belief did not come by any process of reason, but through the indisputable power and revelation of the Holy Spirit.

47

During the next several days Ethan went about enthralled with what he would later discover was his rebirth. He did not see Jesus often since He was spending a great deal of time with His apostles. This was all right with Ethan. He was just grateful for any opportunity to see and hear Him. Each time he did, he was more encouraged and his faith strengthened by what Jesus said.

It was a few days after Ethan's conversion when he saw John. They were both overcome with emotion, embracing each other, saying how wonderful it had been and how much they loved Jesus and each other.

John said, "I've really wanted to see you, Ethan. I want to tell you what I've done with the coins."

Ethan replied, "You know John, it's funny, but I haven't even thought about those coins. I don't want to offend you, but I really don't need to know what you've done with them. Those coins for many years were the most important things in my life, other than my family. I don't believe they meant so much to me that I violated the second commandment. They were not a god, but I valued them too much. I know now that their only value was to lead me to Jerusalem and our risen Lord. I told you when I gave them to you that Jesus had told me I would do something good with them. That was not exactly true. He told me that when the time came I would know what to do with them. That time was when I gave them to you.

Whatever good you do with them will be your responsibility, not mine. And you know you'll have to repent for whatever good you do. I've thought about this. It's like burnt offerings. The sacrifice is made to God and nothing of benefit should be left to the one making the offering. King David knew this when he poured out the water brought to him by his mighty warriors from the well at Bethlehem. He said, 'Be it far from me,

O Lord, that I should do this; *is not this* the blood of the men that went in jeopardy of their lives?' I fear my pride if I do anything that benefits me. I truly want to live as King David said in one of his psalms, 'The sacrifices of God are a broken spirit; a broken and contrite heart.' It is me that God wants, not any other sacrifices that I offer."

Ethan suddenly laughed, "You know John, when we were trying to redeem Jesus with those coins, all the while He was redeeming us."

EPILOGUE

Ethan

Forty days after Jesus' resurrection, Ethan and about 500 men and women assembled on the Mount of Olives and watched Jesus ascend into heaven. Even though Ethan was saddened by Jesus' spectacular departure, his heart marveled at its magnificent beauty. There was also great comfort in knowing that Jesus was returning to His glory in Heaven and that one day Ethan would join Him. He was convinced, too, that before Jesus disappeared into the fleecy white clouds above them, His eyes were fixed solely upon him; a lasting memory that Ethan cherished until the day he died.

On the day of Pentecost, Ethan was with many others in Jerusalem when the Holy Spirit came into their midst like a mighty wind in flames of fire, and with amazing power filled them with His presence. Then, after Peter's inspired testimony, over 3000 souls recognized Jesus as the Son of God and accepted Him as their Lord and Savior.

Ethan heeded Jesus' command to be a witness for Him, and afterward he embarked upon many missions to tell others about Jesus and the meaning of His life, death and resurrection. One day when he was with a number of other disciples, he shared with them his experiences that led to his conversion. He told them about the Magi and Joseph, Mary and Jesus, and his showing them the way they needed to escape the dangers that threatened them.

Ethan said, "My friends, I have thought many times about those events, and since I have known my Lord Jesus, I have pondered them even more. God enabled me to show the Magi, Joseph and Mary, with the infant Jesus, ways to cross a mountain in order to escape for a time evil forces that pursued them. Now through our Lord Jesus Christ, God has enabled all of us to show others the way to escape evil forever. I remember so well the first time I saw Jesus after he was grown and heard Him say, 'I am the way, the truth and the life, no man cometh unto the Father, except by me. . . .'"

One of the men exclaimed, "You know, Ethan, you are so right! That is exactly what we are doing, showing others the way. We are all united in this one cause and I think it should have a name. I would propose that it be called 'The Way'." This proposal was unanimously approved by the group, and thereafter, wherever they went, they were known as "The Way."

Ethan lived out the remainder of his life as a devoted follower of Jesus Christ and, when he died, Jesus became his Way into God's Kingdom, just as He had promised.

John

On Golgotha Ethan believed that Jesus spoke to Mary, his mother, and John, but he could not understand what He said. Jesus did speak to them, having said to his mother, "Woman, behold thy son!" To John He said, "" Behold thy mother!"

John clearly understood that Jesus was entrusting Mary to his care and from Golgotha John took her to his home where she resided until her death. In making practical application of Jesus' Parable of the Talents, John invested the three coins and, from their earnings, Mary was able to live very comfortably. After her death the investment of the coins continued to prosper, and its profits met numerous needs of the early church. John lived to be nearly a hundred years old and very ably managed these funds for many of those. Moreover, the endowment of the coins and the good it did continued long after his death.

Judas Iscariot

We know that after betraying the Lord, Judas attempted to undo the evil he had done. He went to the Temple and offered to return the thirty pieces of silver to the chief priests on the condition that they would free Jesus. They scornfully refused. Judas threw the coins down on the Temple floor and went out and hanged himself. The chief priests took the money and purchased a field which would be used to bury those who could not afford a burial plot. Such burial places are known as Potters Fields.

Judas was lost from the beginning. Even had he not betrayed Jesus he was hell bound. He was a thief and a scoundrel, completely under the evil influence of Satan.

<u>Peter</u>

In a much less malevolent way, Peter, by his denial of Jesus, also betrayed Him. Yet he truly repented and was forgiven. More importantly, he did learn why Jesus changed his name from Simon to Peter, which by definition means a "rock." Jesus had told him it would be upon him His Church would be built. This was decisively proven at Pentecost. Inspired by the Holy Spirit, Peter delivered a powerful sermon, resulting in more than 3000 converts. These, of course, provided a firm foundation of the Church for which Jesus himself was the cornerstone.

Peter spent the rest of his life spreading the gospel and building churches. His life ended as did so many others in the early Church, who in spite of persecution, championed their faith in Christ. Peter was eventually tried and convicted by Roman authority and sentenced to be crucified. Tradition holds that considering himself to be too unworthy to be crucified as Jesus was, he requested to be crucified upside down. His request was granted.

It might well be, however, that Peter's request was made to signify that Jesus Christ had indeed turned the world upside down.

HE IS RISEN

He is risen! He is risen!
Sing it loud and plain,
Till all men o'er the earth,
Hear the glad refrain.

WHEN He arose,
He conquered death and sin,
And planted hope and peace,
In the hearts of men.

SINCE He arose,
He is seated by God's throne,
Making constant intercession,
For those who are His own.

BECAUSE He arose,
We too, shall rise.
When He comes again,
We'll meet Him in the skies.

He is risen! He is risen!
O let the truth resound;
Tell this wondrous story,
Wherever man is found.

Alice Barbour Bennett
(The author's mother 1899-1996)